BORDEAUX CHATEAUX

A HISTORY OF THE GRANDS CRUS CLASSÉS

1855–2005

All photographs reproduced in this book are by Christian Sarramon,
with the exception of the following images:

Page 18 (bottom): Archives de Château Latour
Page 19: © Musée national de la Marine/L.-S. Jaulmes
Page 21: © Archives du Domaine Clarence Dillon SA
Page 22 (left): © Roger-Viollet
Pages 28–29: © Max Alexander
Page 301: © Guy Charneau
Page 315: © François Laforêt, Archives du bureau de courtage bordelais Tastet & Lawton

Translated from the French by Louise Guiney and Susan Pickford

Copyediting: Linda Gardiner

Typesetting: Thomas Gravemaker, Studio X-Act

Proofreading: Slade Smith

Color Separation: Penez Édition, Lille

Cartography: Édigraphie, Rouen

Distributed in North America by Rizzoli International Publications, Inc.

Simultaneously published in French as *Grands Crus Classés 1855–2005*
© Éditions Flammarion, 2004
English-language edition
© Éditions Flammarion, 2004

26, rue Racine
75006 Paris

www.editions.flammarion.com

05 06 07 5 4 3 2

FC0458-05-V
ISBN: 2-0803-0458-5
Dépôt légal: 10/2004

Printed in Italy by Canale

BORDEAUX CHATEAUX

A HISTORY OF THE GRANDS CRUS CLASSÉS

1855–2005

PREFACE BY HUGH JOHNSON

TEXTS BY JEAN-PAUL KAUFFMANN, DEWEY MARKHAM,

CORNELIS VAN LEEUWEN AND FRANCK FERRAND

PHOTOGRAPHY BY CHRISTIAN SARRAMON

Flammarion

May this book remain a testimony of thanks to the generations
who came before us as well as to the directors, heads of culture, and vineyard and
wine-making experts, who devote themselves every day to ensuring that the wines
of our Grands Crus Classés 1855 are different and unique each and every year.

PHILIPPE CASTEJA

President of the Conseil des Grands Crus Classés
du Médoc en 1855

Editor's note: This book presents only those Chateaux from the 1855 classification of Bordeaux wines that produce red wines and members of the Conseil des Grands Crus Classés du Médoc en 1855.

Contents

Some charterhouses, like Branaire-Ducru, shown here (preceding page), were already surrounded by vineyards long before the pivotal 1855 classification. The tasks people performed there, like those immortalized by Jean Dunand on this lacquer bas-relief, were considered almost sacred (facing page).

A Fundamental Document

By Jean-Paul Kauffmann

Truth and authenticity usually go hand in hand with simplicity. The sheer superiority of Bordeaux wines has a lot to do with the elegant simplicity of their classification. It is a completely clear system which does the job it was designed to do perfectly. It possesses all the power of persuasion and conciseness which such transparency brings, giving Bordeaux wines a unity and a harmony of style that other regions can only admire enviously. Thanks to the classification system, the wines of Bordeaux were the first to attain the status of an ideal as a symbol of harmonious order. They set the standard. The hierarchy of Bordeaux wines has inspired other wine-makers to emulate their example, just as the Order of the Round Table spurred knights on to ever greater deeds of chivalry. To develop the metaphor, we might compare the sixty or so wines that have stood the test of time and fully deserve their place on the list to the Knights of the Round Table, representatives of a heroic and selfless way of life and defenders of ancient and noble traditions. While men are born and die, these wines have remained constant. Since 1855, the owners of the châteaux have upheld their sacred duty, devoting their lives to the service of producing great wines whose glory will outlive them. Yet the honor comes with a heavy burden of responsibility. Lower the standards for even a moment, and the system will be unforgiving.

These great wines, whose names echo through the halls of fame, must constantly strive to maintain their level of excellence if they are to continue to enjoy their privileged status. The sense of duty shared by the wine-growers who continue to honor a promise made some hundred and fifty years ago goes a long way to explaining the respect in which the classification system is held. The system is only possible because all of the winegrowers are constantly aware of the need to uphold its values. And indeed, it is reassuring to note that while some châteaux have known disappointing years, none have ever truly let the side down.

In this day and age, when transgression has become a virtue and virtual reality is encroaching on our daily lives, many people are nostalgic for the values of the past. The 1855 classification was the fruit of years of careful consideration and observation, and thus represents a certain stability and dependability—qualities sorely lacking in today's world. It is tempting to see the classification, which some have compared to the elegant solidity of classical architecture, as a monument of the past, venerable, distinguished, but in the end irrelevant. But it should be borne in mind that the classification was not dreamed up as a vainglorious celebration of the qualities of Bordeaux wines. It was a serious experiment aimed at exploring the mysteries of wine production—an inquiry which has continued to the present day. Bordeaux is the first truly modern wine. It owes a great deal of its modernity to the classification, which is first and foremost a masterpiece of rational pragmatism, reflecting the state of the market in an evaluation process lasting almost half a century and resulting in a degree of authenticity that has often been imitated but never equaled. This authenticity is the fruit of the perfect understanding the winegrowers have come to have of their soil. The classification is a reflection of this perfect understanding. If the classification were to be drawn up again today with the same criteria, the end result would be practically identical.

The Bordeaux winegrowers often talk of the classification as if it were an old family friend. The group of châteaux has taken on a distinct, almost human, identity. The wines share a common bond of quality, but each has its own particular character. True skill lies in reconciling the two requirements—individuality against a background of shared characteristics. In the Bordeaux classification, the division of the wines into five groups is absolutely self-evident. Each wine is a building block in the edifice of the classification as a whole. Winelovers have been trying to improve on the classification for a hundred and fifty years. Wine writers and experts of all sorts spend hours in animated discussions on the question. Yet rather than being weakened by this questioning, the classification is simply strengthened as the impossibility of improving on it becomes ever more apparent.

It is rare for such a system—it was drawn up on the orders of Napoleon III—to still be in operation a century and a half later. The 1855 classification was designed to be perfectly adapted to the Bordeaux wine region. Long may it remain so.

THE MÉDOC:
THE CLASSIFICATION
OF 1855 TODAY

By Hugh Johnson

Today the landscape is as orderly as a garden—a garden on the grandest scale where the allées are innumerable, the bosquets are small forests and the eyecatchers are large houses, but this is unmistakably a landscape where productivity is allied with pride and pleasure.

Four hundred years ago it was very different, *un pays sauvage et solitaire* where the few villages were separated by worthless marshy ground, where a few vines, fruit trees, and crops along with many animals supported a population linked only by the great gray river ebbing and flowing between the distant mountains and the sea nearby.

Little suggested that fortunes lay buried in its soil, or that within three generations a Médoc proprietor at Versailles would be wearing buttons on his coat made from the polished pebbles of his own land—the habit, we are told, of Nicolas-Alexandre, Marquis de Ségur, proprietor of Châteaux Lafite, Latour, Mouton, and Calon, known as the "Prince of the Vines."

The Médoc was ripe for development, strategically placed between the city of Bordeaux and the sea where its merchants made their living. The itch for land is not uncommon among men who spend their time in the court and the counting-house. That they had not been tempted to look north to the Médoc was due to its notorious marshes; that they changed their minds, to the Dutch.

The visitor to the Médoc today traverses plateaux of serried vines like vast, gently contoured dunes. Between and around them avenues of poplars criss-cross low-lying ground. The terrace of Château Lafite surveys a noble *potager*, then poplars, then a gravel hill of nursery-slope pitch crowned by an essay in chinoiserie: Cos. The perfect fitness of both slopes, the first in Pauillac, the second in Saint-Estèphe, is guaranteed by the grassy interval, where the Jalle du Breuil carries its water calmly seaward. Look at a map of the Médoc. It is punctuated by these watercourses, embroidered between with lesser ditches and these in turn by buried drains—all the work of the Dutch *desiccateurs* of the seventeenth century.

Drainage brought the land to life, and is still the only link between soil and wine quality that science can prove. Instinct and experience worked together to lead the first investors to the highest points in this unemphatic landscape. They cleared farms and orchards and woods to plant cuttings of a dozen different vines. At random? Far from it. A bush telegraph was at work, notes were being compared, alliances formed … to do what? The goal was better wine: wine for a more mannered, more polished society. Bordeaux was a mass of scaffolding as it tore down its medieval houses and rebuilt in stone. The same philosophy was being applied in the country; replacing rudeness with refinement; finding a new idiom for civilized and reasonable living.

*A trio of still empty glasses, magnified by the artist's lens,
projects a foretaste of fully balanced enjoyment.*

There was no model. How should the vines be planted, trained, pruned? Which varieties were best? Should they be fed with manure? When should the grapes be picked? How crushed and fermented? How long should the juice rest on the skins? Should the winepress be used? What barrel should they use? How long should they wait before bottling? And what scents and flavors would define success?

The Médoc was planted for profit, rather than for the pleasures of country-house life. Its best produce was chiefly destined for a foggy and not very friendly island to the north whose ruling class would pay any price, it seemed, for sweet-drinking wines. Initially it was only the "first growths," first in time as well as in quality, that appeared on this novel market. Then the seconds, from *domaines* planted as close to the firsts as possible. Then by degrees a dozen, then another dozen, and another, of aspirants, establishing themselves on what was left unplanted of the auspicious soil. Until, within little more than fifty years, every susceptible site in the communes of Margaux, Saint-Julien, Pauillac, and Saint-Estèphe, and many more north, south, and west, had been colonized by the vine.

The Médoc is an eighteenth-century settlement, perhaps begun earlier, certainly finished later, but born in the Age of Enlightenment and hence more rational than extravagant. The emphasis is on production; the buildings that matter are the vatrooms and barns devised by eighteenth- and nineteenth-century technology. Two of its châteaux, Margaux and Beychevelle, are architecturally ambitious; the rest are just as much as was needed to dignify the marque and offer hospitality to clients and comfort for the owner's family. Often this involves the seaside chivalry of turrets, but nobody is fooled.

It is this fitness for their purpose that gives the châteaux their unity and their attraction. They seem dedicated more to Apollo than to Dionysus: order and elegance are their priorities. From the parade-ground dressing of a hundred identical barrels in the *chais* to the sober wallpaper and upright armchairs in the *salon*, there is nothing over-stimulating to the visitor's senses. As the photographs in this book brilliantly demonstrate, the little details say it all …. The shining bottle is produced, its visiting-card label is inspected, and the ruby liquid cascades into the crystal glass.

Yes, it is emphatically the wine: redder than a ruby, deeper, more lustrous. Its scent combines the sea-girt land and its fruit, sweet currants and gritty earth, pale oak staves, and even the nacreous Atlantic light, into a memory-trigger as strong as roses. And its power as it washes the tongue, a strangely ascetic draft, comes from ripeness held in a precisely calculated grip of astringency, warm and cold at once, as much a puzzle as a statement. Wine that satisfies soul and body together.

This was what the merchant-growers found in the soil, recognized, and perfected. They knew their palette was limited. The variables are nuances of climate (the closer to the river the more moderate), the proportions of gravel, sand, and clay determining drainage, and the consequent selection of Merlot and Cabernet. And, of course, time. In this respect the clients are players, too. They can hit, or they can miss, the glowing glorious moment (a long moment, true—several years, in fact) when a great vintage is in full song. They can also find joy in the minor key of a poor vintage well made.

There remain the ambitions, the energy, and the competence of the proprietor. Bordeaux possesses an ancient computer—the combined experience of the brokers who fine-tune its trade. In 1855 it produced a famous printout. A hundred and fifty years later it is not the last word, but it remains the first.

No matter where you are, the North is said to begin just after the next village. However, it is the Saint-Estèphe countryside (above and preceding double page) that marks the true northern boundary of the Médoc region, often shrouded in mist. The famed Lafite-Rothschild estate, although adjacent to the boundary, belongs to the Pauillac appellation (facing page).

150 YEARS OF EXCELLENCE

By Dewey Markham Jr.

T he history of Bordeaux may be read in the pages of its classification. More than just a hierarchy of wine-producing estates, the list speaks volumes about the origins of the region, the wine trade that makes it function, and, of course, the châteaux themselves.

Bordeaux's geographical location shaped its commercial destiny from its earliest days. Situated on the banks of the Garonne river, the city was founded as a Roman outpost where wines from inland regions upriver were loaded onto ships headed back to Italy. Later, when vines were planted around the city and the area became a major wine producer in its own right, the region's production followed the same ocean-bound route to its markets overseas. This was especially necessary since domestic sales for these wines faced a significant problem. The French customers for wines of this caliber were to be found among the nobility at court in Paris; however, Bordeaux's distance from the capital was a major handicap in their acceptance, since it meant that numerous taxes and tariffs were placed on the wines as they made their way north. Vineyard areas closer to Paris, such as Burgundy and Champagne, tended to be more popular because fewer charges were imposed on them, resulting in a relatively lower price.Given the international nature of its market, by the seventeenth century there were two main buyers for Bordeaux's wines: the Dutch and the British. Each customer was fundamentally important, albeit in very different ways, in shaping the character and quality of the wine we enjoy today.

The Dutch sought out the cheapest wines they could obtain, with quality being a secondary consideration. Since their purchases were destined to be shipped to Dutch colonies throughout the world, whatever finesse a better-quality wine might have possessed would have long disappeared by the time it reached its destination. To help preserve the wines during their long voyages, Dutch merchants developed a number of techniques to give them greater potential for successful aging. For example, burning sulfur in a barrel before filling it with wine enabled the contents to arrive in a more drinkable condition. (Of course, it would be several centuries before Louis Pasteur's discovery of bacteria as the agents for the wine's spoilage. The Dutch had no way of knowing that sulfur acted as an antibacterial agent—all they knew was that the wine benefited from this

There is nothing more meticulously exact than a great Bordeaux wine dealer's ledgers.
The ledgers of Tastet & Lawton are shown here.

The same wigs, the same velvet bands, the same ermines—and yet, more than half a century separates the opulent entertainments of Arnaud III de Pontac (above, top) from the follies of Nicolas-Alexandre de Ségur, dubbed the "Prince of Vines" (above, bottom). Both, however, were familiar with these Bordeaux docks immortalized by Vernet for the "Ports de France" series (facing page).

treatment.) Thanks to such methods, the Dutch gradually transformed Bordeaux from a wine to be drunk quickly to one that was capable of a marked improvement with age.

Bordeaux's other major customer was substantially different in its orientation. The British put their purchases on ships that made a relatively short voyage north, where they drank all the wine themselves. Accordingly, their main priority was better quality, and the vogue for these wines among the upper-middle class became so great that a continually increasing demand inexorably drove prices ever higher.

In the 1640s, it was sufficient for these wine drinkers merely to ask their merchants for a wine from the Médoc region to be assured of obtaining something of superior quality, and price lists from this period show that Bordeaux's production was classified according to such large, regional divisions. However, with the passage of time, customers' requests became more and more focused, homing in on particular communes that had developed commercial reputations for better wine-making techniques. By the middle of the seventeenth century, contemporary price lists show that Bordeaux wines had become identified not just as Graves, for instance, but also as Pessac.

As the decades passed, British wine drinkers became more precise in designating the origins of their wines, and from the commune level attention shifted to individual producers who had developed a particular reputation which set them apart from their neighbors in the same locality. This process is generally acknowledged to have begun with a commercial initiative by Arnaud de Pontac, the owner of Haut-Brion. During the rebuilding of London in the wake of the Great Fire of 1666, de Pontac sent his son to the English capital to establish a tavern known as the Pontac's Head that would serve as a showcase for the wine from his estate. The tavern—and the wine—became quite fashionable with London's middle class, and the identity of a wine's producer began to gain greater significance when making a purchase. By the end of the seventeenth century it was no longer sufficient to ask for a Pessac; now drinkers instructed their merchants to acquire Haut-Brion.

Haut-Brion was not the only property that benefited from this early "brand awareness" among British wine drinkers. Three other properties had also carved out a distinct identity for themselves in wine drinkers' consciousness: Margaux, in the commune of the same name, and Latour and Lafite, situated in Pauillac. Because the quality of the wine from these four producers gave them unparalleled name recognition, demand for them was higher than for any other wine, and this demand caused their prices to achieve a level unmatched by any other property in Bordeaux. Together, Haut-Brion, Margaux, Latour, and Lafite were grouped in their own commercial category, which came to be known as the "first growths."

By the middle of the eighteenth century other producers, who saw the financial rewards that such efforts at quality brought, also sought to make wines that would be worthy of note among the higher-paying British wine drinkers. A group of properties succeeded in creating a similar recognition for themselves in the marketplace, albeit without ever achieving the very highest prices that the four first growths had managed to win. These properties, whose wines were closely grouped together in price, became known as "second growths." Around a dozen vineyards were generally acknowledged as being in this category. However, a number of additional properties were beginning to break free from their communal anonymity, although they had not yet achieved the clear commercial identity of the four first growths or the group of second growths which followed them.

By the time Thomas Jefferson arrived in Bordeaux in the spring of 1787, this system had evolved to encompass a well-defined third growth level. Their commercial success encouraged the identification of yet another series of wines as a category only slightly inferior to the third growths. Price lists from the 1820s show that this trend continued with the establishment of a fourth-growth level. By the early 1850s, there were five well-defined classes in this commercial hierarchy, comprising some sixty wine producers.

Thus it was that the structure of this commercial ranking system took form, developing from the top down and continually evolving as conditions at the individual properties and in the Bordeaux marketplace changed.

In the early 1600s, the wines most in demand were from the Graves, but as the century progressed and the Médoc developed its vocation as a top-quality region, its wines developed a greater following—and their prices rose accordingly. By the middle of the nineteenth century, the Médoc wines commanded prices so high that Haut-Brion remained the only wine that could match them, and thus became the sole Graves property worthy of inclusion in the upper ranks of this hierarchy; none of Bordeaux's other red wine regions produced anything that could match these prices.

The classification was a cornerstone of the local wine trade, and everyone involved—merchants, proprietors, and brokers—knew where each property was situated within it. This familiarity with the established pecking order was reinforced by the wide distribution that the classification came to enjoy. From its primary use among initiates of the Bordeaux wine trade, the classification found ever-wider exposure throughout the nineteenth century in a great variety of venues. Wine books destined for wine drinkers were becoming more common in the early 1800s, and the list was often incorporated in the text, in books like *Topographie de tous les vignobles connus*, by André Jullien in 1816; *The History of Ancient and Modern Wines*, by Alexander Henderson in 1824; and *A History and Description of Modern Wines*, by Cyrus Redding in 1833. The classification also demonstrated its utility in helping to shape public policy: it was included in a British Parliamentary report "On the Commercial Relations between France and Great Britain" drawn up in 1835, and in a survey commissioned by the French Minister of Agriculture and Commerce entitled "Vine Growing, Evaluation of the Produce for 1847 and 1848." The evolving list even made appearances in a growing number of tourist guidebooks for visitors to the region, such as *Le guide de l'étranger*, which went through several editions beginning in 1825, as well as an 1846 work entitled *Bordeaux: Its Wines, and the Claret Country* by Charles Cocks (which eventually became

MOUTON

Bᵒⁿ DE ROTHSCHILD, Propriétair

1858 ←———————

Galos

Gérant

~ BORDEAUX ~

Bordeaux et ses vins, the "bible" of Bordeaux). With each new appearance in print of the wine trade's classification, proprietors, brokers, and merchants all saw how the price structure of the marketplace currently stood, and consumers gradually developed an increased appreciation of the idea of quality in Bordeaux wine.

As personally satisfying as it was for producers to see their properties achieve classed-growth status, there was a more practical aspect to this system for the Bordeaux wine trade. Each spring when a new vintage was ready for sale, buyers and sellers alike were faced with the task of determining a just price for the wines on offer. As the principal industry in France's biggest department, the wine trade was a large, complex enterprise whose very existence depended on its smooth operation. With thousands of producers offering wines for sale to hundreds of merchants, the entire system would have collapsed if buyers had to begin arranging prices from scratch each year. The classification was a well-refined tool which served to streamline the process.

Based firmly on a property's track record of sales prices over an extended period of time, the classification offered a shortcut in commercial negotiations, a starting point from which an appropriate final price for a wine could be determined efficiently. If a property had traditionally sold its wines at the third-growth level, for example, and others in this class were getting a hundred francs per bottle, both the proprietor and the potential customer knew that a price of around a hundred francs was a fair estimation of the wine's commercial value, and negotiations could begin with that as a point of departure.

It was (and still is) habitual for proprietors to hold back the release of their new vintage until they were able to see the level of acceptance or resistance which that initial asking price met with in the marketplace. There was no fixed order of precedence in the declaration of prices, and the system enabled the Bordeaux marketplace to develop the level of efficiency that was essential for the world's largest fine wine region to operate smoothly.

In 1855, a Universal Exhibition was planned for Paris, and goods from all over France—and the world— were shipped to the French capital for display. Wine was sent from Bordeaux in a collection organized by the city's Chamber of Commerce. However, the organizers faced a tricky problem: only six bottles of each wine were to be sent to Paris, a quantity sufficient merely for the display and for a private tasting by a panel of judges. The thousands of ordinary visitors to the Exhibition would not have the opportunity of tasting the wines to develop an appreciation of the different qualities possessed by Bordeaux's wines. All that would be evident to these masses would be the rather ordinary sight of a uniform collection of bottles lined up on the shelves of a display case. To render the presentation more interesting and to better communicate the idea of superior quality represented by Bordeaux's best production, a wine map of the region was commissioned to accompany the display. As part of this map, a roster of the finest wines from Bordeaux was included, and the Chamber of Commerce asked the Union of Brokers to furnish a list of the properties that were worthy of such status. The brokers were the ideal choice for the job, since among the three main actors in the Bordeaux wine trade—producers, brokers, and merchants—they were the only ones with a comprehensive view of the entire commercial picture. The proprietors knew their wines better than anyone, but their appreciation of the larger picture beyond their vineyards was less authoritative. The merchants had a good understanding of the market for Bordeaux's wines, but commanded a lesser knowledge of conditions at the properties. Only the brokers had a first-hand knowledge of production, developed through their scheduled visits to the vineyards throughout the year, and a well-developed sense of a wine's commercial prospects, thanks to their greater proximity to the marketplace.

Thus it was that on April 5th, 1855, the Chamber of Commerce addressed a letter to the Brokers' Union requesting a "list of all the red classed growths in the department, as exact and complete as possible, specifying to which of the five classes each of them belongs and in which commune they are located." Due to the impending debut of the Universal Exhibition, which was less than a month away, a tight deadline was imposed. The brokers had all the necessary sources on hand to supply the list of the best wines in such a short time. On April 18, they produced the list, which has become known as the "1855 classification." One hundred and fifty years

During the period when Talleyrand (above, top) owned Haut-Brion, this grand cru had not yet won official recognition. The 1855 classification followed the Exposition Universelle, to which Napoleon III welcomed Queen Victoria—as shown in this fine tapestry from the Mouton collections (above, bottom).

Neither President Jefferson (above, left), nor wine dealer Lawton (above, right) needed the kind of confirmation afforded by the 1855 classification (facing page) to appreciate wines from the Médoc. There are some, like these two men, who are capable of anticipating official approval.

after its drafting it remains one of the most authoritative references in the world of wine.

A property's inclusion on the list did not result merely from furnishing the Chamber of Commerce with wine to send to Paris; indeed, most of those on the list did not bother to send samples. (A close look at the original document shows that the word *point*—meaning "none"—is written across the names of those properties that did not offer wine for display at the Universal Exhibition.) A property's inclusion in this hierarchy was also not a result of making a superior wine in 1854 and getting an abnormally high price that year—and, consequently a place in the classification in 1855—followed by a return to inferior quality in succeeding vintages. The ranking system of Bordeaux's wines was based not on one year's results, nor even a half-dozen or so vintages; it was a long-term track record that earned a property its berth in the classification. If there was a sole reason why the properties appearing on the 1855 classification were included, it was simply because they deserved to be there. Their superiority was established by a consistent level of exceptional quality over an extended period of time that left no doubt as to their fundamental capacity for producing great wine. With time this brokers' list achieved an authority and a longevity that the more ephemeral versions prior to 1855 had never achieved. Throughout the latter half of the nineteenth century, this classification became the accepted, authoritative source for understanding the notion of quality at the top end of Bordeaux's production. However, it must not be thought that this status as a reference for wine drinkers prevented the trade from continually reevaluating the just price for a property's wines, based on its current performance. The genius of the 1855 classification is that it has never hindered the continuing functioning of the wine trade in its task of ensuring that the quality of a wine finds its commensurate recompense in the marketplace. Thus, even though the brokers' classification has experienced only two official changes since its transcription in April 1855—the promotion of Mouton Rothschild in June 1973, and the inclusion of Cantemerle among the fifth growths on September 16, 1855—the quality of a property's wine has always encouraged mobility in its current price, earning it an appropriate position above or below its "official" 1855 ranking.

The brokers' judgments from 1855 remain remarkably accurate; however, no one would argue that their classification continues to present the same precise picture of the wines' relative quality as it did one hundred and fifty vintages ago. Today, the classification's greatest role is as a promotional tool, not only for the properties it includes, but for the greater Bordeaux area. No other wine region possesses a similar system for ranking its wines with a renown equal to that enjoyed by Bordeaux's classification. As a basic road map to the finest wines that this vineyard area produces, the classification offers a reliable and reassuring, reference for novice wine drinkers when making their initial selections. The words "1855 Grand Cru Classé" constitute a guarantee that the bottle bearing this legend will offer a winethat will do a host proud when it is presented to guests.

On the hundred and fiftieth anniversary of the 1855 classification, it is evident that the world of wine is richer for the existence of this testament to the outstanding quality of which the Bordeaux region is capable. The list itself and the names inscribed upon it have achieved a double existence that speaks to both our spirits and bodies: a mythic status that speaks to the possibility of achieving perfection in an imperfect world, and a tangible expression in the form of the wines themselves, which offer so much pleasure to oenophiles everywhere.

Chat: de Beychevele	St Julien	L. F. Guestier S.
Le Prieuré ...	Cantenac +	N. Pages
Marquis de ...	Margaux +	Oscar Sollberg

Cinquiemes Crus

Canet	Pauillac	de Pontet
Batailley	@	L. F. Guestier Son
Grand Puy	@	Fre: Lacoste ainé
Artigues arnaud	@ +	Duroy
Lynch	@ +	Twine
Lynch Moussas	@ +	Vasquez
Dauzac	Labarde +	Wiebrol
Darmailhac	Pauillac +	
Le Tertre	Arsac +	H. Cerry
Haut Bages	Pauillac +	Liberal
Pedesclaux	@ +	Pedesclaux
Coutenceau	St Laurent +	Bruno Devez
Camensac	@ +	L. Popp

AN EXCEPTIONAL *TERROIR*

By Cornelis van Leeuwen

The 1855 *grands crus classés* owe their exceptional character in part to the efforts of the winemakers over the decades, but also largely to the exceptional qualities of the *terroir*. *Terroir* is a French word from the Latin *territorium*. Yet *terroir* means much more than just the soil in which the vine grows. It refers to all the characteristics of the vineyard that influence the finished wine, such as soil, climate, exposure to the sun, and so on. The *terroir* is the bond between the bottle of wine and the place that made it what it is.

Winemakers were aware of the influence the *terroir* could have on the quality of the wine as early as Roman times. In the Bordeaux region, the notion of the *terroir* was developed in the Middle Ages, when wines were named after the village where they were grown. Evidence survives to show that prices varied according to the village, suggesting that some villages had a reputation for producing better wine than others. Already we can see an as yet very primitive hierarchical classification emerging in the Bordeaux region. In the Middle Ages, however, judging the quality of wines was a far more hit-or-miss affair than today, because all of the wines from the same village were sold at roughly the same price, independent of their quality. It was not until the seventeenth century that the notion of individual estates began to emerge. In purely chronological terms, Château Haut-Brion was the first estate to sell its produce separately. As a result of this change, the notion of the *terroir* became much more clear-cut, as the place of origin of a wine would now be traced to within a few acres on an individual estate rather than the thousands of acres that a whole village's vineyards might cover. Perhaps surprisingly, the English wine market played a decisive part in this development, as the English were prepared to pay high prices for excellent wines, and one way of guaranteeing consistent high quality was to identify the *terroir*.

The famous philosopher John Locke visited Bordeaux in 1677, and wrote an account of his travels in the region. This account is a valuable source of information on how contemporary winemakers understood the effects of the *terroir* on the wine. Locke's voyage to the Bordeaux region was akin to a pilgrimage—so impressed was he by the quality of the Haut-Brion wines he had drunk in London that he decided to go and

The "Bordeaux Mixture" (an insecticide)—the result of experiments conducted by David and Millardet from Dauzac—covers vineyards, such as Pontet-Canet, shown here.

see the estate for himself. He noted that the owner of the estate explained that the superb quality of his wine was due to the porous, gravelly soil and good slopes, light composting, and old vine stocks. These are precisely the qualities recognized as producing the finest wines today. It is amazing to think that over three centuries ago, winemakers had already discovered this.

John Locke's journey also illustrates the remarkable traceability of wines from the great *terroir*s, like the wines included in the 1855 classification. Whereas *vins de marque*—vintage wines—are blends of wines from various estates, a *vin de terroir* will always be made of grapes grown on one single estate. This is what gives it its principal characteristics and qualities, and it also means that wine lovers can visit the vineyard, admire the very vines that produced the *grand cru classé*, and talk to the winemaker who produced it. Nowadays, the issue of traceability has become vital in the food industry as a whole, but the 1855 classification recognized its importance a century and a half ago.

The growth of the vine and the ripening of the grapes are very dependent on weather conditions such as the average temperature, rainfall, hours of sunshine, and wind. Vines are extremely vulnerable to cold snaps, unexpected late frosts, and hailstorms, which can destroy a crop representing a year's labor—not to mention income—in just a few hours. The quality and character of wines are greatly influenced by the weather. The word *terroir* includes this notion of the vine's sensitivity to the prevailing weather conditions.

For the grapes to ripen, the vine needs warmth and light. If the weather is too hot, the grapes will produce too much sugar. They can still be used for wine, but the high sugar content is bad for the taste. According to the well-known wine experts Ribéreau-Gayon and Peynaud, if the weather is too warm, the grapes ripen too quickly, burning up the essences which give great wines all their finesse. In other words, the best wines are produced in regions that enjoy clement weather, sufficiently warm to ripen the grapes, but not so hot that they reach maturity too quickly. The climate in the Médoc region is perfect for winegrowing. The average annual temperature is 55°F (13°C), and 68°F (20°C) in July and August.

The average rainfall is less important. Grapevines are very adaptable, capable of surviving extreme droughts. They can be cultivated without the need for irrigation in regions with an average of just sixteen inches (400 mm) of rainfall annually, as long as the water does not drain away too quickly. They will also adapt to very wet conditions where the average rainfall can be as much as forty inches (100 cm). However, in such conditions, the vine will put its energy into growing shoots rather than building up sugars in the grapes, and fungal diseases will be harder to prevent. The average annual rainfall in the Médoc region is thirty-three inches (850 mm), slightly over the level where grapes attain the perfect sugar concentration. However, this is not a problem because the soil allows ample drainage.

The Médoc is rarely affected by hailstorms, probably because it is not a very hilly region. The Atlantic seaboard and the Gironde estuary regulate the climate to a certain extent so that the region is hardly affected by unexpected rises or drops in temperature. Late frosts are an unusual occurrence. In 1991, for example, a terrible late frost hit the Bordeaux region in the night of the 20 to 21 April. The *crus classés* from estates lying along the banks of the Gironde, such as Château Latour, were relatively unaffected, and went on to produce wines of excellent quality that year.

Weather conditions in the Bordeaux region can vary dramatically from one year to the next. This results in a marked variation in the quality and character of the wines, depending on the year the grapes were harvested. This is why the question of the vintage is so important. The wine's character reflects the weather

The islet of Trompeloup, lying in front of l'Ile Philippe, is one of the many delightful surprises to be found on the Gironde, a river as broad as an estuary.

in the year it was bottled. Wines tell us that the years 1945 and 1947 had long, hot summers that produced great vintages, that 1963 and 1965 were very rainy—so wet, in fact, that many winegrowers did not even bother to bottle the weak, insipid wine under the estate label. Quite apart from the question of the quality of the wine, the vintage is a way for each estate to produce a different wine each year while maintaining the particular style for which the *cru* is appreciated. The vintage is a way of exploring various facets of the *cru* with each grape harvest. In years like 1978 and 1988, when the summers were rather cool, the grapes ripened slowly and the harvest was later than normal, giving the grapes more time to develop their aroma and producing a wine of great finesse. Hot summers like those of 1982, 1989, 1990, and 1995 give powerful wines. Since average rainfall in the Bordeaux region is slightly higher than the ideal level, it is perhaps unsurprising that all of the greatest vintages were harvested in years when rainfall was below average for the region in the months from June through September.

Several thousand grape varieties are cultivated throughout the world. Each variety is the result of careful crossbreeding by generations of winegrowers to develop certain characteristics, such as early or late ripening or ideal sugar content. However, just a few dozen of these varieties are considered suitable for use in truly great wines. The grape variety must be capable of adapting to the prevailing weather conditions, especially the time the grapes take to ripen fully. An early ripening variety in a hot climate will produce mature grapes earlier than elsewhere. They are harvested in August—or February in the southern hemisphere—and will have a high sugar content, but will be lacking in freshness and the aromatic compounds that give great wines their subtlety. On the other hand, a late-ripening variety planted in cooler northern climes may not produce ripe grapes at all and will produce an acidic, grassy wine lacking in color. Part of the reason the *grands crus classés* of 1855 are so outstanding is that the grape varieties are perfectly adapted to the prevailing weather conditions, ripening at exactly the right moment, except in unusually cold years such as 1972. The grapes ripen slowly, allowing them to develop the aromatic compounds that give the wine its rounded body. This perfect harmony of grape varieties and weather conditions is very difficult to achieve. The same grape varieties in a slightly warmer or cooler climate will produce a different wine altogether. The 1855 *crus classés*, like other Bordeaux wines, are the result of a careful blend of grape varieties. The art of choosing complementary varieties is what give the wines their stunning complexity. Expert winemakers vary the proportion of grapes used in a wine to balance out the less desirable qualities of each variety.

Cabernet Sauvignon is held to be the most noble of the grape varieties. It is the most widely used variety in the 1855 *crus classés*. Some seventy percent of the vineyards that produce the First Growth *crus classés* Margaux, Latour, Lafite-Rothschild, and Mouton Rothschild are planted with Cabernet Sauvignon. It is a relatively late-ripening variety, and in order for the grapes to reach their full potential, the vines must be planted on the very best soil that will speed up the ripening process. It gives average-sized but fairly regular yields. The bunches and the grapes themselves are relatively small. It will not produce a very high sugar content, but the ripe grapes are rich in color and tannin. Cabernet Sauvignon produces aromatic wines dominated by dark fruit such as blackcurrants while the wine is still young. After aging, the wine takes on an extraordinary complexity of aromas, notably with notes of cocoa and mint.

Merlot grapes are nearly always used alongside Cabernet Sauvignon. This variety is planted on a third of some vineyards such as Haut-Brion and in a few cases, such as Palmer, half the land is given over to it, the other half being planted with Cabernet Sauvignon. It ripens around two weeks earlier than the Cabernet Sauvignon variety, which means it reaches maturity every year even when the weather is cool, when Cabernet Sauvignon will struggle to ripen. Merlot is better adapted to wetter ground conditions. But to allow it to reach its best, its natural generosity must be curbed. Merlot produces colorful, sugary grapes with full-bodied tannins. When young, the predominant aromas are red and dark fruits, which develop into candied

The neat parcels of land in the Saint-Julien and Pauillac vineyards (preceding double page), as on other Médoc estates, are planted with four varieties of rootstock: cabernet sauvignon (facing page), for the most part, with merlot, petit verdot, and cabernet franc (above, top to bottom).

fruit, leather, and fur as the wine matures. Merlot wine tends to age a little faster than Cabernet Sauvignon wine.

Cabernet Franc is the third most important red grape variety in terms of surface area in the Bordeaux region. It is more at home in the Libernais than the Médoc, although no one has yet quite fathomed why. It ripens later than Merlot, but earlier than Cabernet Sauvignon. Some people find its taste too light, but it is capable of great finesse. Some *crus classés* have succeeded in producing outstanding Cabernet Francs on very old vines in ideal soil conditions.

Just a small proportion of the Bordeaux vineyards is planted with Petit Verdot, but this variety plays a key role in some vintages. It is a late-ripening variety, which means the wine it produces varies in quality from year to year depending on the weather. As the signs all indicate that the global climate is getting warmer, we should expect to see more and more Petit Verdot vines being planted in the region in the years to come. It is a difficult, demanding variety that needs to be planted in conditions that will encourage the grapes to ripen as soon as possible, with a moderate amount of watering that must be carefully judged not to deprive the vines of the precious liquid they require. Once these conditions are fulfilled, Petit Verdot gives a very rounded wine that could almost stand on its own without blending.

After the climate and the grape variety, the soil is the third factor that goes to make up the *terroir*. The roots of the vine draw all the water and nutrients the plant needs from the soil. Soil conditions can vary a great deal depending on the texture, gravel and mineral content, the capacity to hold water, and the depth of the soil layer. As Dr. Seguin, a specialist at the Faculty of Oenology at Bordeaux University and an acknowledged expert in soil types, has established, there is no one ideal soil type. The quality of the wine depends on the interplay of a number of factors. Having said that, certain characteristics are indispensable to grow good quality grapes.

The mineral content of the soil varies greatly from one place to another. The winegrower can add mineral fertilizers as he sees fit to enrich the soil with the nutrients it lacks naturally. As a general rule, the best winegrowing soils are not over-rich in minerals. In the Médoc, the mineral content of the soil is often reduced by the presence of large quantities of flint and gravel which do not feed the soil. No research has yet succeeded in proving the direct influence of any given chemical element on wine quality.

The winegrower may need to water his vines if the soil allows the rainfall to drain away too readily. This is a vital factor in wine quality. The ideal is to reduce the vine's water intake during the summer, halting the growth of the branches and the grapes themselves and producing a high concentration of sugars. However, too little water, and the grapes will simply not ripen fully. This is an extremely rare occurrence in the Bordeaux region, mainly affecting very young vines whose root system is still very shallow in the course of unusually dry summers.

As the Bordeaux climate is rather rainy, the best way of limiting the vines' water intake is to plant them in well-drained soil. The best Médoc soils are perfect, as they have a very high gravel content. Because the rainfall rapidly drains away, the soils warm up easily in the spring sunshine, encouraging the grapes to ripen quickly. This is particularly important in vineyards planted with a late-ripening variety such as Cabernet Sauvignon.

Gravelly soils are common to all the *cru classé* estates. These soils are warm and help the grapes ripen quickly. The water drains easily from them and they make it possible for the winegrower to control the amount of water taken up by the vines and thus improve the quality of the grapes. The wines grown on gravelly soil are rich in tannins and are best left to age for several years. They often boast exceptional finesse, particularly when Cabernet Sauvignon is the principal grape variety. Some of the finest wines in the 1855 classification, for example Château Latour, have vines that grow on very clayey soil. This type of soil often

The essence of the Bordeaux region's magic is concentrated—distilled, as it were—
in the soft lights sparkling on the little port of Pauillac.

The remains of crushed stems lying between rows of grape vines (above) and early morning dewdrops glistening on trellised vines (facing page)—two sights familiar to those who like to linger in vineyards.

produces the best grapes, although few winedrinkers associate Médoc wines with clay soil. The real advantage a clay soil offers is to allow the grower to control the wine's water intake, giving powerful wines with full-bodied tannins. All four principal grape varieties can be grown on clay soils.

The Bordeaux region also has some clay-limestone soil, particularly in the Margaux appellation around the village of Saint-Estèphe and in Haut-Brion. Clay-limestone soil is excellent for vines, but it retains water better than gravelly soils, which means the grapes ripen a little later. It is therefore best suited to growing Merlot, producing powerful wines with a relatively high alcohol content that complement wines grown on gravelly soils superbly in blends.

The 1855 *crus classés* are often grown on sandy or sandy-gravelly soil. Patches of sandy soil mostly lie at the foot of gravel outcrops or on the western fringes of the region, where they can be rich in humus. Vines grown in these soil conditions tend to be vigorous and give an abundant yield. The winegrowers control this vigor by limiting the amount of fertilizer used and sowing grass between the rows of vines to draw off some of the nutrients. This allows them to produce excellent wines, particularly with Merlot grapes. When young, these wines are bursting with fruit notes. Since they age quickly, they are especially suited for use in blends of *seconds vins*, the second wines that many of the great châteaux produce alongside their principal output.

Each type of soil in the Médoc has its own unique characteristics. The grapes that go into the 1855 *crus classés* are grown on several different types of soil. After harvesting, the grapes are vinified in different vats according to the type of soil. This means that the same fermentation cellar can produce wines with strikingly different personalities. During the blending process, the winemaker will play to the strengths of each to produce a wine that draws on the best features of each variety. The result is far more subtle and complex than each grape variety could produce on its own. The rest of the harvest generally goes to make the second wine, which can be an excellent way of discovering the *crus classés* without breaking the bank.

The exact blend that goes into a *grand cru classé* varies from year to year, as the grapes grown on each soil type react differently to the prevailing weather conditions. The diverse range of soil types and the size of the estates are in fact a major asset for the winemakers, giving them a lot of scope to produce the finest blends possible.

The *terroir* is a subtle harmony resulting from the effects of the soil, the weather, and the grape variety, skillfully combined by the winemaker. Other parts of the world share conditions and soil types similar to those found in the Bordeaux region. Cabernet Sauvignon grapes, which owe their reputation to the excellence of the 1855 *crus classés*, are now grown all over the world. But what makes the 1855 *grands crus classés* so unique is the remarkable harmony of the soil, the climate, and the grape varieties. Cabernet Sauvignon grapes are brought to perfect ripeness by the Bordeaux climate, as long as the soil is warm enough to hasten the process. The well-drained soils draw off the excess rainfall and prevent the vines from taking up too much water, building up sugar levels in the perfectly ripened grapes. But the *terroir* would be nothing without the expertise of the master winemaker. It is entirely due to the efforts of generations of skilled vintners that this southwestern corner of France has become one of the greatest winegrowing regions in the world.

PORTRAITS OF THE CHÂTEAUX

By Franck Ferrand

Without standards, there could be no Bordeaux wine, no style.
Standards keep alive all that is pure and timeless.

Jacques Chardonne

Coming from the city of Bordeaux to the Médoc region, you feel as if you have reached the end of the world. It is a long, thin peninsula and, as the locals say, from the far end of the spit of land you can just about make out France across the estuary. The mists that roll up the Gironde—the River, as the locals call it, with a capital R—the square fishing nets set up here and there, the eels that live in the shallows, the wood pigeons that are a local specialty in season, the great stretches of land barely above sea level with just the occasional hillock, the vines that cover the land like a cloak—this is the soul of the Médoc region. And then there are the châteaux. What would the Médoc be without its châteaux?

It is as if a giant has scattered handfuls of toy castles across the landscape, all landing neatly in the folds of a vineyard. They are more or less extravagant in design. Some are ostentatious, while others are delightfully modest. Some are converted charterhouses, founded by monks who worshipped there for centuries. Others are uninhabitable, merely for show, to look pretty on a wine label. Nearby, you will always find the rows of imposing buildings indispensable for the running of a modern vineyard—the cellars and storehouses. Each of these buildings has a specific, well-defined function—fermenting or aging the wine—but they also serve the common purpose of impressing the visitor with the vast array of high-tech equipment used in winemaking today. The winemaking facilities at Château Margaux, for example, could almost be compared to a stage set, with certain features picked out with dramatic lighting. Some are built in the form of a rotunda, like the cellars at Château Pichon-Longueville, or an amphitheater, like Château La Lagune. In recent years, architects who were called upon to work on plans for the cellars where the wine is aged in casks have also come up with some remarkable designs. The world-renowned architect Ricardo Bofill designed the superb cellars at Château Lafite-Rothschild; the cellars at Château Talbot and Château La Tour Carnet are also striking.

All of this magnificent architecture is dedicated to the greater glory of Bordeaux wines. It has to be said that since the local villages are rather ordinary, the châteaux play a vital role in forging the cultural identity of the Médoc region. Their superb reputation has made them the defining symbol of a whole way of life and has proved a great boon for the local economy. Pick up any guide book of the Bordeaux region and you will find a large proportion of its pages devoted to wine tours and tastings. Driving along even the smallest roads in the Médoc, you will come upon countless signs pointing you to the nearest château. Although today, the market for fine wines suffers from two problems—unscrupulous speculators who buy up wines in the hope

This glimpse from a window at Lascombes beautifully expresses the feeling
of intimacy reigning over most of the region's wine-growing estates.

of reselling them at a vastly increased price in a few years, and the hectic pace of life, which means that fewer and fewer people can take the time to savor the wines as they deserve—the winemakers believe that teaching people about fine wine is a way of investing in the future.

By and large, the owners and managers of the estates are always pleased to welcome visitors and show them around the buildings and vineyards. Some have become wellknown at a regional and even national level, and could even be called legends in their own lifetimes, such as Alexis Lichine and Baron Philippe de Rothschild. Others are continuing the sterling work begun by their illustrious predecessors—the names Jean-Michel Cazes at Château Lynch-Bages, May-Eliane de Lencquesaing at Château Pichon-Longueville, or the Comtesse de Lalande spring to mind. These well-known names are ambassadors for their estate, while an army of managers, oenologists, and other employees, down to the grape-pickers in the fields, work behind the scenes, devoting their time and their expertise to the greater glory of the wine. Some have climbed their way up the ranks to join the exclusive club of the best wine experts in the world. It is undoubtedly a good thing for the Médoc to allow these men and women of talent to prove their worth. The old aristocratic families have recognized that their estates can safely be entrusted to the graduates of the excellent winemaking and vineyard management schools in Bordeaux and that their long-standing traditions can benefit from new ideas.

Most of the estate managers and owners now speak at least two languages fluently—a sure sign of the increasing interest in Bordeaux wines all over the world. While it is still the case that the biggest market for the finest Bordeaux wines is France, and three-quarters of exports are to other European countries, it should be borne in mind that the Médoc has a long history of exchanges with other countries, dating back several centuries. It is not uncommon to see the flags of other nations flying over the vineyards—Château Kirwan has links with Denmark dating back many years, Château Batailley likewise with Austria.

Yet the success of the Bordeaux estates cannot be explained by the friendly charm of their owners, nor by their international links. There is no denying that the 1855 classification still gives an extra touch of *je ne sais quoi* to the reputation of Bordeaux wines. Of course, like any institution that is a century and a half old, the classification has had its share of ups and downs. It was only in the early 1980s, for example, that the American wine guru Robert Parker and his followers revived the fortunes of these sixty châteaux, which had suffered in the post-war years in many cases, helping them to reach even greater heights of quality and, in some cases, sheer glory. From then on, things have gone from strength to strength.

The winemaking tradition in the Bordeaux region dates back a thousand years. Over the centuries, trends have come and gone, but one has remained constant—the need to create the perfect balance between the *terroir* and the aging process, growing the grapes and blending the wine. Today, vintners tend to stress the importance of intuition in the winemaking process, believing that you have to *feel* when the moment is right, when the grapes are perfectly ripe, when the blend is the best it could be. As a result, the focus today tends to be on making the best of the *terroir*. Some estates even have three-quarters of their employees working on this aspect of the winemaking process. Great wines require exceptional soil conditions—something that only Nature can provide.

The task of the winemakers can thus be summed up as making the very best of the *terroir* they are blessed with, and making sure its finest qualities shine through in the finished wine. Their work can be compared to that of top chefs who select the finest ingredients and then marry their qualities to produce a dish that is greater than the sum of its parts. I also like to compare them to virtuoso musicians who follow the score but interpret the emotions of the piece in their own unique way. And to continue the analogy, since every season is different, each vintage is like a variation on a well-loved theme.

In an exotic tower photographed at Cos d'Estournel (bottom) and a salon snapped at Le Tertre (facing page), one perceives all the refinement of extraordinary estates.

Unlike fine wines from other regions, Bordeaux wines are differentiated by vintage and not by the blend of grape varieties. Each bottle is a concentrated essence of all the hours of sun and the rain squalls that brought the grapes to perfect ripeness. In the words of the wine expert Jacques Perrin, "Apart from the pleasure they give us when we taste them in the full ripeness of age, these wines are a marvelous way of traveling back in time."

In the olden days, it was frequently said that Bordeaux wines would be good in December if the weather had been fine in London in August. These days, things are a little more complicated. Expert winemakers can make up for shortcomings in the *terroir* to a certain extent. But they are not miracle-workers. As I watched the master winemakers at work, I marveled at their evident love of their job and the care and attention they lavished on the delicate fruit. Their gestures are always gentle and never brusque. They cradle the bunches of grapes as lovingly as if they were new-born babies. Humility and a sense of deep tradition are vital qualities in a master winemaker. They have to be perfectly attuned to the region's traditions, some of them centuries old, which have proved their worth over generations. The great winemaking tradition in Bordeaux is made up of countless tiny improvements discovered and incorporated into the process year by year.

The greatest changes in the last half-century have been the mechanization of many of the tasks in the vineyard formerly carried out by employees, the replacement of horses by tractors, the introduction of steel fermenting vats—as early as 1961 at Château Haut-Brion—and the first scientific studies of the genetics of the grape family and soil composition, as at Château Palmer and Château Durfort-Vivens. The most recent innovation has been the development of techniques measuring phenol levels.

It is inspiring to read the history of all these châteaux. The novel *Le Vin de la liberté* (*The Wine of Liberty*) by David Haziot recounts the history of life at the Château Cos d'Estournel from the days of the French Revolution to the early twentieth century. Apart from the changes in winemaking techniques, the novel describes beautifully the deep-rooted rapport between the men who work on the land and the vines they tend. This rapport is one aspect of the winemaking process that never changes. There is something deeply human about working in harmony with the soil and with nature. All of the winemakers I have had the privilege to meet say that they love working to produce something which gives people so much pleasure. For what could be nicer than uncorking a bottle or two to share with friends? As one of them put it, "Wine is more than a work of art—it is something made to be shared. It is definitely one of the finer things in life."

It is true that many of the winemakers I spoke to in the course of writing this book had something of the philosopher about them. Maybe it is the constant contact with nature that gives them such wisdom, or maybe it is spending so many years learning patience and discipline, waiting for the right moment to pick the grapes, to blend the varieties, to put a stop to the fermentation process. Such decisions require great confidence in one's own abilities and a finesse not given to everybody.

Having written this book, I feel I have a far better understanding of why the race to produce ever better wines worthy of their *appellation* has not led to a greater degree of rivalry among the owners of these estates. I understand that what matters is not being the best, but making the best of what the estate has to offer.

The greatest quality of Bordeaux wines is their balanced, elegant, refined classicism. So the result that the winemakers strive to attain is discreetly classic rather than spectacular. This ideal marries well with the Bordeaux countryside—a land of harmony, serenity, and plenitude.

Château Lafite-Rothschild

Château Latour

Château Margaux

Château Mouton Rothschild

Château Haut-Brion

CHÂTEAU
LAFITE-ROTHSCHILD

Pauillac

He who pales among the highest will shine among the second-highest," wrote Voltaire in his infinite wisdom. What he meant was this: that being the highest, in any realm, implies the possession of unique qualities and exposure to great risk—or, as British humorist Saki put it, with the witty cynicism that was his trademark, "The top Christian always gets the biggest lion." The "lions" here, under the skies of the Médoc, are clothed in the ultracivilized garb of wine critic, oenologist, and gourmet. They can be good, bad, or indifferent—but none should be trusted implicitly.

Lafite has occupied the highest position, without interruption, ever since the sacrosanct 1855 rankings were first published. Preeminence indeed, but with its own risks. Lafite is still a legendary name on five continents and furthermore one that is easily pronounceable in any language. Lafite: a name that inspires dreams everywhere, a mythical estate boasting physical assets so extraordinary they are hard to imagine. Lafite stands on the finest hillocks of Pauillac, a series of mounds formed by deep layers of fine gravel that

benefit from an ideal exposure. This is soil blessed by the gods, and the wine made from grapes grown on it represents, in the world of the connoisseur, an absolute standard of perfection: full-bodied, subtly aromatic, intense in color but not too strong to overwhelm its faint notes of almond and violet.

In its three great centuries of existence, Lafite has basically belonged to only two families, the Ségurs and the Rothschilds, linked somewhat haphazardly to a family of peerless managers, the Goudals. There have thus been three dynasties associated with this foremost name among all the *grand cru* wines ranked in 1855.

Credit must be given where credit is due: at the Ségurs's, the man who deserves credit for having established the quality and consolidated the standing of the divine beverage is obviously the illustrious Nicolas-Alexandre. But the hazards of history have also played their part, and the Bordeaux physician who in 1755 prescribed a cure of Lafite for the Marshal-Duke Richelieu, the new governor of Guyenne, surely deserves a place among the estate's

*The unerring Rothschild taste has for many years
left its mark on the salons at Lafite.*

benefactors. "Excellency," Louis XV is said to have remarked to Richelieu on the latter's return to Versailles, "I am tempted to believe that you are twenty-five years younger than when you left for Guyenne." To which his faithful courtier is supposed to have replied, "Sire, Your Majesty must no longer be kept in ignorance of the fact that I discovered a fountain of youth there. It is a generous, delicious cordial, comparable to the ambrosia on which the gods of Olympus sup." Thus was the great Lafite wine launched; thus did its Golden Age begin. After this incident, Lafite was served at the royal table, and at many others. Then, and long afterward, the "Prince of the Vines" could rightly boast of supplying the "King's wine."

Lafite did not enter the Rothschild orbit until much later—well after the 1855 rankings—when it was purchased by Baron James Rothschild in the summer of 1868. However, the baron died shortly after he made his purchase, and the following autumn the property was inherited jointly by his three sons: Alphonse, Gustave, and Edmond. The ensuing years ushered in a second golden age for the estate, with record prices for a series of exceptional vintages. The eminent family's task was to extract the wine's maximum potential during good years and limit the damage during less good ones. The worst ordeal they faced was no doubt the grave crisis afflicting French vineyards as a whole at the end of the nineteenth century, when the dual plagues of mildew and phylloxera struck. The outbreak of the World War I complicated the management of an estate that was labor-intensive. The blow sustained by Lafite during the World War II, twenty years later, proved almost fatal. The estate was occupied, requisitioned, and nationalized. When the Rothschilds recovered their property in 1945, it

Here, by placing the casks around a grandiose rotunda, Ricardo Bofill has designed what amounts to a temple dedicated to wine.

projects that grandiose image that distinguishes it from its imitators, it is doubtless owing to this attentive spirit. The baron sought to go even further, however. He wanted to associate the name of Lafite in the public mind with those of great contemporary artists. This led to the idea of having the estate portrayed through the lenses of some of the century's leading photographers, including Jacques-Henri Lartigue, Irving Penn, Robert Doisneau, and Richard Avedon.

In 1988 an idea with more serious implications was to endow the physical site with the finishing touch it had heretofore lacked. Baron Eric, expressing his desire to raise the estate to even greater heights, took the daring step of commissioning Catalan architect Ricardo Bofill to design new aging cellars. The morning the blueprints arrived, rolled up inside a large architect's tube, a small group of the faithful gathered for the unveiling were left speechless by what they saw. And, indeed, Bofill's idea was a wild one—but a very "Rothschild" one, when you stop to think about it. He had designed a circular room in which the casks of wine would be arranged in concentric circles around a skylight rotunda. A brilliant, transcendent idea, the kind generated only as major projects near completion and which, through a combination of aesthetic power and obvious practicality, add that touch of magical inevitability so often associated with the most elegant concepts.

Today the Lafite cellars have become one of the great architectural curiosities of the Bordeaux region. It would be a mistake to miss seeing them, but just as much of a mistake to stop there. Nothing, in fact—even a architectural concept—should for an instant overshadow that which, by virtue of its ranking and the unanimous opinion of the critics, must continue to stand above all else. We mean, of course, the wine: the divine nectar, the "elixir of youth," taken in itself and for itself.

had deteriorated drastically. The family decided to entrust the youthful Baron Elie with the task of reviving it. The energetic new master, a charter member of the Commanderie du Bontemps du Médoc, succeeded in restoring both vineyard and winery, once again achieving almost incomparable quality, and also, thanks to an excellent marketing policy, winning market share at a time of continually increasing competition.

In 1974 it was the turn of Elie's nephew, Eric de Rothschild, to take over the leadership of an estate which by then was definitively freed from the rut in which it had been mired for so long. The estate's new master respects tradition and knows how much his great wine owes to the virtues of the distinctive Rothschild style. The winery resembles the stables of a British stately home; the deep, dark cellars are like ancient catacombs. All of this contributes to enhancing the image of a noble heritage. But Eric de Rothschild also knows the importance of technical facilities in both vineyards and winery for maintaining the excellence of Lafite. Using effort and imagination, he is establishing the conditions for the creation of a third golden age—one that will be even more golden, perhaps, than the two others.

Eric de Rothschild, "a vintner by inclination, a banker by obligation," is one of those aesthetes who definitely "never takes frivolity lightly." For him, the smallest details are the objects of meticulous attention; and if the property today still

*The spirit of a great estate is not only projected
through the refinement of highly elegant decors
(preceding double page and above) but also lurks
in the studied obscurity of a fine cellar (facing page).*

CHÂTEAU
LATOUR

Pauillac

Images of Château Latour's crenellated tower surmounted by a heraldic lion figure majestically on the estate's cases, its labels, and even on the white tissue paper in which each bottle is wrapped prior to shipping. An emblem as timeless, regal, and universally recognizable as a chess piece. In fact, however, the original donjon-like structure that first gave its name to the most prestigious estate in the Médoc region is no more. Not a single vestige remains of the imposing fourteenth-century structure, then known as La Tour Saint-Maubert, which served as the main living-quarters in a fortress erected during the Hundred Years' War. The charming little edifice standing today under peaceful skies, endowed with the courtesy title of "tower," is actually a dovecote built in the time of Louis XIII.

However, whether or not the "tower" is really a tower is considered irrelevant by connoisseurs of great wine; the main interest of the estate lies, not in its architectural features, but in its land—a semifluvial area adjacent to the Gironde, blessed with a rising contour ideal for vineyards and exceptionally fine soil mixed with river gravel.

This outstanding estate's major assets are geological. The vineyard's 160 acres (65 hectares), including a 116 acres (47 hectares) of extremely homogeneous land constituting the famous "Enclos," benefit from an ideal microclimate, a peerless exposure, perfect drainage, and a soil quality most vintners can only dream of. With a foundation such as this to work with, how could anyone go wrong?

For example: during the great freeze of 1991—a major disaster—losses for most local vintners were about seventy percent, but the figure was only thiry percent at Latour. Was this a miracle? Is Latour beyond reach? There are many people willing to believe it is, especially since the discovery in the 1960s of estate archives going very far back in time (some date from 1331), which tend to confirm, and even magnify, the miraculous aspect of this centuries-old good fortune.

The foremost figure in the history of Latour is the Marquis de Ségur, a man with a magical touch when it came to vineyards. Known during his lifetime as the "Prince of the Vines," early in the eighteenth century he pioneered methods of extracting maximum benefit from an extraordinary

This ancient dovecote—the estate's signature, in a way—casts
its dark silhouette onto the glimmering Gironde at sunset.

potential, creating a "Latour style" that has remained uncontested down to our own day. Subsequently, according to numerous meticulously annotated estate registers, the property was managed by a series of men who reverently adhered to rules laid down by its founding father. It is safe to say that the reputation of the great Château Latour *cru*, which quickly spread to England and even the New World, remained unchallenged until the golden age inaugurated by the 1855 rankings.

Other events on the estate, occurring nearer our own time, are worthy of note, events reflecting the general evolution undergone by the region's *grand cru classé* wines over the past half-century or so. For example, when the British Pearson group acquired Latour from the flagging descendants of the Marquis de Ségur, the estate—despite its flagrant obsolescence—was still producing great vintages, including the admirable wine of 1961. Nonetheless, systematic modernization was called for. The new British owners proceeded to initiate a genuine *aggiornamento*.

Additional parcels of land to the west of the ancestral estate were planted; an artificial drainage system was installed to supplement the work of nature. Even more dramatically, the estate's new masters mechanized and automated work in the vineyard, and replaced the old wooden fermenting casks with stainless steel—an unheard-of heresy at the time. And yet there was no diminution in the wine's quality. If anything, it improved. The years 1966, 1970, and 1975 (among others) were again notable for the production of wine well above accepted standards of excellence.

When the new owners assumed control, they also supported a policy of massive exports in response to the traditional British taste for French "claret." The acquisition of Château Latour by the British came as no surprise to seasoned observers of the Bordeaux wine trade. It was both a sign of the times and the logical outcome of local developments. Thus did a gem among the vineyards of France pass into the hands of foreign investors, where it stayed for over thirty years—until Breton entrepreneur François Pinault

The central section of the vineyard is known as "l'Enclos" (right).
The décor of the tasting room draws its strength from a
combination of spaciousness, transparency, and reflected light
(following double page).

younger people can be highly motivated by the virtual certainty that they will live to see the results of their decisions over the long term. It may be noble to work for something that only generations as yet unborn will see, but it hardly affords the same satisfaction.

The new vitality perceptible indoors is just as pervasive outdoors as well. Many lovers of Latour must bitterly regret not having enough years still ahead of them to sample some of the vintages that have not matured yet, but will in time. As the elderly Mazarin is said to have remarked on contemplating his antique collection and wine cellar: "To think I must leave all of this behind me! To think this wine will age without me!" A lament surely echoed by many a despairing connoisseur today.

Patience and confidence in the future are two virtues etched in the genetic heritage of Château Latour. It should be pointed out that this *premier cru classé*, which ages particularly well, is made to defy the passage of time. Meanwhile, however, consumers are becoming increasingly impatient and undisciplined. They want to drink it *now*. This problem is dealt with at Latour by offering their best customers facilities for storing wines at the estate, in the purchaser's name, until the day comes when the wine is fully mature and ready to be "liberated."

This is a sterling example of judicious planning for the future, through a system in which the vintner acts, basically, as a banker. The wine is purchased by the customer, but left for safekeeping with the vintner, who releases it only at maturity, at the exact moment when the passage of time will have transformed a delicious liquid into a timeless nectar—the noblest and most transcendent of human creations.

eventually acquired it in 1993. This was the moment when a new chapter in the Latour saga opened.

"We're fully conscious of the estate's brilliant past," explains estate manager Frédéric Engerer, "and we're proud of it. But the past is the past, and now we need to look ahead and deal with the obstacles in our path. My vision of Château Latour is a vision of the future." This attitude might seem disconcerting at a vineyard with such a storied past, but it's actually a continuation of that past: Médoc vintners have always looked ahead.

A philosophy focused on the future is perfectly consistent with the new owner's personality. François Pinault's love of everything new—and particularly of modern art—is common knowledge. A visit to the innovative winery installed in an extension built onto the cellars provides a persuasive demonstration of the fresh approach being applied to Château Latour—an approach that is resolutely modernistic and streamlined, almost Zen-like. Large expanses of charcoal gray, clean lines cut by right angles, and mineral tones of cement, granite, and glass combine to create a futuristic setting totally new to this region.

In his vast, uncluttered, efficiently organized office, the manager elaborates: "We're lucky. Our team is young, with plenty of energy and drive. We hired our top people in 1999, and most of them are in the thirty-something age group—a big advantage." Youth may not be everything, but

The tower topped by a lion is visible everywhere—on the temperature regulation panel, in the fermenting room (top left), and even on the large cellar windowpanes (facing page).

CHÂTEAU
MARGAUX

Margaux

The Médoc's most famous estate is also one of its most imposing. But to visitors, it belies the old saying that familiarity breeds contempt. Here the opposite is true: the closer one comes, the greater the awe one feels. The farther one advances down the sun-drenched avenue bordered by venerable plane trees, the farther one advances toward this temple of great wine, this magnificent theater of oenology, the stronger the spell it casts. Familiarity does not necessarily breed contempt; and, despite the words of the French poet, some heroes do remain heroes, even to their valets. Some myths—rare ones, to be sure, but all the more notable for that—can withstand close scrutiny without losing any of their ability to amaze.

When visitors climb the twenty-two steps to the monumental entrance flanked by a cleanly designed and unornamented ionic peristyle with pediment, they have the almost palpable impression of witnessing the legendary name's grandeur materialize before their eyes. By virtue of an ancient royal privilege, Margaux is the only château to bear exactly the same name as the wine produced on its land.

Once at the top of the stairs, visitors enter the vast and luminous vestibule and pass through immense doors to salons furnished in imperial style. By this time they fully realize that everything here is larger than life. "The privilege of the great," wrote Jean Giraudoux, "is to contemplate catastrophes from the safe distance of a terrace." The privilege of guests at Margaux is to admire the most famous vineyard from the high windows of a residence that is truly royal.

The person reigning over this splendor is a youthful woman as noble and devoid of superfluous frills as the setting, which suits her perfectly. Corinne Mentzelopoulos is determined to be a worthy heir of the eminent gentleman from Patras, Greece who—having made a fortune in distribution—had the wild idea of bidding for this French institution. The transaction took place in 1977. Back then, investing in a vineyard—no matter how prestigious—might have seemed like a strange thing to do. A risky bet, at the very least. André Mentzelopoulos could justly claim to be a man ahead of his time. Just over three years later, on the eve of producing his first vintage wine, the vineyard's new owner

The façade on the garden side of the house, although less well-known than
the one on the courtyard side, is also a testimony to Bordeaux neoclassicism.

died. "My father didn't live to see the fruit of his efforts," laments his daughter. She speaks feelingly, an eloquent revelation of the source of her own devotion to this spot.

Before he died, however, André Mentzelopoulos did have enough time to instill a new spirit at Margaux—a burgeoning spirit that eventually spread to all the Médoc vineyards. The many innovations reflecting this spirit included land drainage, recourse to outside consultants for advice on operations, replacement of many old casks with new ones, and the excavation of a spectactular cellar—a first in the Médoc—one perfectly adapted to the aging of the wines in the cask. These initiatives were imitated and copied until, ultimately, they became the general rule. Spearheading a major battle, if not a revolution, Mentzelopoulos had completed the *aggiornamento* of Margaux at least two years before even his nimblest colleagues began theirs. He was a trailblazer, and many followed in his footsteps.

His daughter sees herself as the custodian, more than the heir, of this legacy. She doesn't say, "Margaux belongs to me," but rather, "I belong to Margaux." As this city-bred former specialist in literature admits with a touch of gracious false modesty, "I'm not even a native of the Bordeaux region." She goes on to explain that she thinks of herself as half Greek, a little American, and above all , a Médocan.

And yet, without striking a blow, she has completely conquered the exclusive little world of local vintners. Her dedication, her respect for the field, her humility before an infinitely complex art, have won her admission to a society traditionally suspicious of newcomers. Above all, however, this woman—who in 1980 was very young indeed—earned the acceptance of her peers by demonstrating her unwavering determination to concentrate all of her energies on Margaux. Her first step was to seek the necessary support.

Whether felt from afar, in the vineyard
(left), or from up close, in the treasure-trove
cellar (preceding double page), the spirit of the place
is the same—haunting, inimitable.

Next, she set out to regain full control over her property. This led her, first, to an alliance with Giovanni Agnelli of Turin, and then to acquisition of a majority shareholding from her family. Blood will tell.

Corinne Mentzelopoulos is quick to recognize her debt to the united, energetic team around her. The group's major asset is clearly youth. "In the beginning," recalls Corinne, "most of us were less than thirty years old." This was true, notably, of Paul Pontallier, who manages the estate under her supervision and serves as her trusted deputy in the field.

This warm, affable man leads visitors from surprise to surprise on a tour of the sumptuous winery, which is built above and below ground around a courtyard as vast as a city plaza. It was André Mentzelopoulos's idea to bury the huge vaulted winery joining the two main buildings. The result is a succession of rationally planned rooms leading from the magnificent wooden casks to the coopers' workshop—one of the last in the *crus classés*. The oldest cellar is an immense room joined with an imposing, monumental, unadorned ionic colonnade: a masterpiece of pure design and worth the trip for itself alone.

"This is one of the most beautiful wineries there is," Paul Pontallier emphasizes. "When we arrived, it looked exactly as it does now, in all of its purity, and we were careful not to change it in any way. What you see today is what you would see in photographs taken here in the nineteenth century."

From architecture to philosophy is but a step, and at Margaux that step is easy to take. Nowhere else could one better address the basic question of innate versus acquired characteristics, nature versus nurture, force versus form. Nevertheless, we must abandon abstract intellectual conjecture and return to earth, to the physical source of all this—and how sensual it is! At the end of our grand tour, Paul Pontallier pours a little nectar into large, generous glasses. The tasting—or demonstration—takes place in undisturbed silence. Depth, breadth, strength . . . "No doubt about it," he murmurs, "this is 2003 a great wine. A great wine: the kind you'd rather savor than talk about."

As evening falls on the pure and elegant courtyards of Château Margaux and it is time for visitors to take their leave, they feel a change in themselves. Drawing away regretfully, under the mist of a light rainfall, they cast one final glance over the brightly lit façade of the colonnaded manor receding in the distance, at the end of the long avenue lined with plane trees. It is time to leave Margaux; time, sadly, to return to the world outside.

The cluster of estate buildings (above),
which even boasts a cooper's workshop (facing page),
is like a small old-fashioned village.

CHÂTEAU
MOUTON ROTHSCHILD

Pauillac

Popular belief notwithstanding, the most famous "Mouton" in the world is totally unconnected with the succulent lamb raised in Pauillac. In old French, the word *mouton* referred to the modest *motte* or hillock on which one of the greatest wines of the Médoc is still produced today. The play on words was irresistible, however. Baron Philippe de Rothschild, who was born on April 13, 1902 under the astrological sign of Aries (the Ram), couldn't resist this opportunity to associate his name with a subtle reference to his powerful tutelary animal.

Baron Philippe was only twenty years old when he inherited a joint share in the ancient fiefdom of Brane-Mouton, first acquired seven decades—and three generations—earlier by an ancestor from the London branch of the family, Baron Nathaniel Rothschild. For the youthful heir—man-about-town, member in good standing of the Parisian elite, ebullient aesthete fascinated by English poetry, and a lover of auto racing and travel—retiring to the depths of the Bordeaux countryside could not have been easy. It took courage and, even more, the depth of passion that people say never lies. The baron's choice of a career was to have incalculable consequences from the very start, not only for the fiefdom of Mouton but for the entire wine-producing sector.

In 1924 the young prodigy caused a scandal when he decided to bottle his vineyard's production on the estate. From then on, all of the great Mouton wine was bottled at the château. With this decision, Baron Philippe brutally wrested from centuries-old local wine dealerships the operations which, until then, had given them the upper hand over vintners. It also meant extra costs for the producer, who now bore a wholly new responsibility—but at the same time enjoyed a wholly new prestige.

As with all revolutions, this one involved change, starting with the estate's buildings, which were too small for storing several years' production. New facilities were installed in 1926, notably the long "main cellar," the first of its kind in

Although this could be a library in Paris, or Sologne—or even Provence—it is actually one of the most popular salons in the Bordeaux region.

the region. Exhibiting his innate sensitivity to visual settings, Baron Philippe commissioned the brilliant Parisian stage designer Charles Siclis to plan the building's interior. The theatrical lighting in this long, vast, uninterrupted space, and the spectacular arrangement of the casks within it, guaranteed the success of a masterly and pioneering installation that has since been copied almost everywhere.

The paradox of successful innovations is that, once they have finally been accepted, they appear self-evident and even easy. However, if we project ourselves back into the context of their time and reflect on the revolutionary design of the installation, we can appreciate the daring and vision of those responsible for it.

"Château bottling" made it possible to personalize the wine's labels and make them more distinctive. Poster artist Jean Carlu was commissioned in 1924 to design the first of them, and he produced a cubist composition combining the symbolic ram's head with the Rothschild family's five heraldic arrows. Following the liberation of France after World War II some twenty years later, the baron chose a design by Philippe Jullian based on the Churchillian "V" for victory.

Many other labels have been commissioned since, many by artist friends of the Rothschild family, including Marie Laurencin, Jean Cocteau, and Léonor Fini. Subsequently, the great wine's labels were designed by a different well-known artist each year, with only rare exceptions:

in 1953, for the centenary of the property's acquisition; in 1977, to commemorate a private visit by the British Queen Mother; in 2000, to celebrate the millennium. This amazing collection of masterpieces was gradually extended with the addition to the list of other famous names—including Miró, Picasso, Dali, Chagall, Baselitz, and Balthus. The artists were paid in kind, with cases of the great wine.

The concept of associating Mouton Rothschild with artwork was expanded during the 1950s with the inauguration at the estate of a museum housing rare objects of fine and applied art from every era, on the theme of vineyards and wine. Opened in 1962 by André Malraux, this collection is unique in the world and has become a jewel of the Bordeaux cultural heritage, amply justifying the regular flow of visitors to a property that is clearly emblematic.

In view of all this, the incentive for Mouton Rothschild to extend its renown internationally was irresistible. The wine merchant—forced by necessity to take the lead as a producer of Médoc *grands crus*—in 1933 launched a second vintage, "Mouton-Cadet," which ultimately became the most widely sold Bordeaux wine in the world. Success breeds success: drastically innovative production, marketing, and promotional methods initiated here eventually spread and were copied by many other vintners.

There remained a wrong that had to be righted. At the time of the 1855 rankings, the authorities had judged Mouton, despite a quality and selling price equivalent if not superior to those of the *premier cru* wines, unworthy of the supreme distinction. This decision was justified at the time by the bad condition of the house and winery. Mouton was ranked first, to be sure, but first in only the *second cru* category! For Baron Philippe, this was an old wound that had never healed. Drawing inspiration from the motto of the Rohan family, he devised his own: "*Premier ne suis, second ne daigne, Mouton suis*"

The sublime lacquerware by Jean Dunand for the Normandy smoking room (preceding double page) elevates the activities of the harvest, just as the label by Jean Carlu immortalizes Baron Philippe's symbolic ram (left).

("First I am not, second I disdain, Mouton I am"). But this verbal retaliation was scant comfort. In his view, the constant improvement in his wine's quality over the span of half a century, the installation of magnificent new facilities, and the prestige won by the château, all combined to justify revision of the original ranking.

It wasn't easy. It took enormous personal energy, an ironclad institutional reputation, and delicate diplomatic maneuvering to combat the solid front presented against him and his ambitions by his competitors—who included some of his neighbors and even cousins. However, in 1973 the baron's stubborn tenacity overcame the dual inertia of the ministry and virtually the entire profession. In a reversal unique in the history of the rankings, Mouton Rothschild was elevated from the category of *seconds crus classés* to the ultra-exclusive club of *premiers crus classés*. The baron then changed his motto to: "*Premier je suis, second je fus, Mouton ne change*" ("First I am, second I was, Mouton I will always be").

Thus unfolded the extraordinary saga of a unique estate, the fame of which is inseparable from the brilliance of the man who over six decades raised it to the heights. When the great man died in 1988, his daughter, Baroness Philippine, assumed control. Abandoning the Parisian theatrical world in order to devote herself to the continuation of a mighty endeavor, this energetic woman showed herself worthy of her father's trust. The same optimism, the same will, the same worldly wisdom—combined with perhaps a more incisive tendency to look outward. The labels, for example, for which she commissioned artists such as Keith Haring and Francis Bacon, bear this out. No true connoisseur anywhere any longer doubts the total commitment of the estate's new muse. Everyone now knows that, for many years to come, Mouton will always be Mouton.

Don't look for a dining room. Here the table is set anywhere,
according to the whim of the moment; for example,
in this charming salon decorated with a frieze of rococo icicles.

CHÂTEAU
HAUT-BRION

Pessac-Léognan

In a country whose history and culture are rich with innovations in the world of literature, arts, and sciences, France's great achievements are evident in such wonders as the ribbed vaults of Morienval and the ageless and famous garden designs of Vaux le Vicomte. Among all of these wonders, Château Haut-Brion must surely take its place as not only the birthplace of the great growths of Bordeaux, but also as the site where the alliance of man and nature gave birth to a new notion . . . terroir! It is easy to understand why a special exception was made for this Chateau in the rankings of the 1855 classification, and why there was no objection to placing the legendary Graves at the very summit of a group containing only Médoc estates. Haut-Brion boasts a number of firsts: the first officially certified appellation, the first estate dedicated solely to the production of wine, the first great wine exported, the first rootstock grafts, etc. The list of innovations implemented by this pioneering estate is endless; as a result, it enjoys a comfortable lead over all others.

The mighty wines of Pontac (as they were once known) owed their primacy to efforts made by the family of the same name. Credit for laying the basic foundation unquestionably goes to the family's distinguished ancestor, Jean de Pontac. A contemporary of Montaigne and La Boétie, he, like them, was a member of the Bordeaux parliament. He became owner of the property named Haut-Brion through marriage, purchased the manor house in 1533, and built the "château" seventeen years later. Through a brilliant stroke of genius, he planted all appropriate land with vineyards, and built his castle on land that was poorly suited for the culture of vines. Jean de Pontac lived to be a hundred years old and remained—according to the archives—"in full command of his good sense, speech, and understanding until he drew his last breath."

The descendants of Jean de Pontac were able to build on the eminent foundations of their forefather. They continued to make improvements on their property, the virtues of which were soon evident in the magical quality of their wine, which became the most complex, subtle and compelling that anyone had ever tasted. A century after the château was founded, the flamboyant Arnaud III de Pontac—the man who built the Maison Daurade (the gilded mansion) in Bordeaux—

This huge stone wild beast apparently roaring into the void
is actually guarding the château's main courtyard.

specifically for the transport of casks, owed its invention to the Northern Europeans' taste for Pontac wines. This introduction to widespread foreign lands of a great Bordeaux wine would pave the way for the commercialization of the wines of the Médoc region. This early status as a wine of international renown has remained with Haut-Brion until this day.

Following the upheavals of the French Revolution and the Napoleonic Empire, the Haut-Brion estate was purchased by a man whose investments were known to be numerous and diverse. This was the Prince de Bénévent—otherwise known as Talleyrand—the indomitable mastermind known to have guided French diplomacy through some of the most epic hours of its national history. Among the numerous and often-repeated legends surrounding the "diable boiteux" (the lame devil) is the story of how, drawing on the genius of his chef Carême, he raised gastronomy to a fine art and made his table an instrument of his diplomacy. What is less well known, perhaps, is that a leading component in this "diplomacy of the table" bore the name of the vineyard acquired by the prince at Pessac. The tradition of combining gastronomy with diplomacy was perpetuated over a century later by a latter-day owner of Haut-Brion, Douglas Dillon, who made it a point of honor to follow the path traced by his illustrious predecessor. Dillon, the United States ambassador to France, supplied the White House and the Elysée Palace with his wine.

The château had been purchased from André Gibert in 1935 by Douglas Dillon's esteemed father, Clarence Dillon. The United States Prohibition laws had only recently been rescinded, and there was an insatiable demand for wine in that country. Clarence Dillon was an eminent New York financier whose flair, charisma, imagination, and longevity evokes the ancestral spirit of Jean de Pontac. An adoptive son of the Bordeaux region, he came late to the world of wine, but approached it with exceptional passion and a keen sense of how important the soil can be. Here was another founding father who succeeded in communicating his enthusiasm to his descendants — as far as the fourth generation, the one which is currently at the helm. Clarence Dillon's granddaughter Joan (later the Duchesse de Mouchy) and his great-grandson, Prince Robert of Luxemburg, seized the torch with all the passion felt for great family enterprises. Today they embody with serene confidence an innate awareness of their mission. The exquisitely furnished château, surrounded by replanted vineyards, breathes a unique spirit—an

Vines dotted with shrubs, an ancient Bacchus with amphora (above); glass with an artful monogram "CHB"— a little bit of magic (facing page).

developed innovative new techniques to market and sell his wines. Just after the Great Fire of London in 1666, a tavern by the name of Pontac's Head was opened and quickly became one of the most fashionable destinations on the banks of the Thames. The English, to their great delight, discovered here the joys of the house wine cited by the inspired Samuel Pepys as "Ho-Bryan."

Another venerable name associated with the estate is that of Larrieu. The Larrieus acquired Haut-Brion under Louis-Philippe in 1836, and they maintained their hold on the property until the era of French president Alexandre Millerand (1922). A sign of the times was the erosion of the power once wielded by the legal profession, which fell into the hands of financiers and bankers. The distinguished Joseph-Eugène Larrieu, the highest bidder in the 1836 sale, was a Parisian banker, very much a part of the Establishment. It is to his son Amédée that the property owes much of its modernization and the wine its preeminence. The Larrieus, father and son, uncle and nephew, continued championing many new winemaking techniques and innovations which allowed their estate to shine.

From the seventeenth century, the wines of the estate were taken on by the English, the Dutch and many others who came to propose new initiatives that would enable the successful and safe export of these wines all around the planet. The "flûte hollandaise," a high-speed vessel designed

overwhelming legitimacy of existence. Haut-Brion is first and foremost an eminent estate lending its name to a great wine.

The proximity of Bordeaux has always been important to Haut-Brion. The Pontacs, who were magistrates in the city, naturally forged links with the great wine dealers. The Larrieus, active in finance, also benefited from their ties to the capital of Guyenne and its society. As for the Dillons, their transatlantic ties prepared them well to benefit from all that Bordeaux has to offer. Today they are privileged to count the university as their neighbor, which facilitates the exchange of information with scholars in agronomy and viticulture.

Agronomy has always been a vital concern at Haut-Brion, the site of early experimentation. The stewards of Haut-Brion were among the pioneers of grafting after the phylloxera epidemic; they brought in machines and tractors soon after World War II, and after the great frost of 1956, they quickly became the champions of selective replanting, opening the door to many avant-garde techniques in the 1970s and 1980s with the participation of Professor Peynaud.

The Delmas family, estate managers—first George, then Jean-Bernard, now Jean-Philippe—have been relentless in their quest for scientific and technical advancement in viticulture, and pioneers in grape varietal research. By isolating a number of genetic families of vines, it became possible to identify clones that had specific and desired qualities. However, abstract scientific research has never been allowed to obscure the essentials. "We have never had either the intention or the desire to make anything here other than a great Château Haut-Brion," explains Jean Delmas. A major focus of research conducted both independently at the estate and in cooperation with the university, is vinification. The first stainless steel fermentation vats in the region were installed here in 1961. These vats are not only more hygienic, they can also be cooled to arrest the fermentation process at the right moment. Forty years after the arrival of these vats, the spirit of scientific inquiry is still dynamic at Haut-Brion, which now boasts vats with inclined bases, the first of their kind. These may be relatively minor revolutions, but they provide the unmistakable evidence of a tradition for innovation. One foot in the past, the other in the future: an infallible rule when it comes to making progress without obscuring the intangible quality of the nectar's soul—that elusive little something responsible for the inimitable and outstanding character of the wine that has come to be known as the "Great Lord of the Graves."

This magnificent vineyard lies in the center of Pessac—which was not yet its location in the eighteenth century (following double page), as can be seen from the wall map (above). Here, meticulous rootstock studies are conducted on the basis of some 370 benchmark clones (facing page).

Château Rauzan-Ségla

Château Rauzan-Gassies

Château Léoville-Poyferré

Château Léoville Barton

Château Durfort-Vivens

Château Gruaud Larose

Château Lascombes

Château Brane-Cantenac

Château Pichon-Longueville

Château Pichon Longueville

Comtesse de Lalande

Château Ducru-Beaucaillou

Château Cos d'Estournel

Château Montrose

CHÂTEAU
RAUZAN-SÉGLA

Margaux

With his salt-and-pepper beard and well-cut jacket, John Kolasa cuts a distinguished figure. He reigns supreme here, the sole authority after God. His poise and presence recall the kind of Shakespearean actors admired in recent years in England for their innovative improvements on the acting style associated with Laurence Olivier. Kolasa projects a maturity ideally suited to inspiring trust and respect in the people who work for him. "I always ask them for their opinions," he explains, "and I put their ideas into practice as often as I can." There can be little doubt that a man like this will see far, and see accurately. His words are modest, however. "I don't go off the deep end, you know. I just do what others did before me."

The context: a comfortable manor house and its outbuildings, adorned—just enough but no more—with topiary shrubs and climbing roses. They compose a picture in which antique tiles, exposed beams, pale stone walls and bell-shaped curbstones project a combination of fantasy and

elegance reminiscent of what's best in old-fashioned cottages. Stately trees add to the picture, as does the admirable view over some hundred and twenty-five acres (fifty hectares) of evenly spaced vineyards. When viewing all this, one can only think that either everything has been preserved just as it was in the past, or else everything has been carefully restored.

The philosophy: the Chanel corporation, who has owned since 1994, has embraced an Anglo-American attitude combining respect for the experts, humility in the pursuit of ambitious goals, and a willingness to work today for the benefit of future generations tomorrow—the unmistakable hallmark of born investors.

The alliance uniting a philosophy, a corporation, and a dedicated individual explains the success of Rauzan-Ségla, and has completely restored its credibility as a leading *second cru classé*. Second only to Mouton Rothschild, decreed the experts of a century and a half ago; yes, and a very close second indeed, confirm the experts of today. If the estate's aim

Mullions, half-timbering, and pendentive turrets—a definite taste
for the picturesque makes its first appearance in the porch.

is to reconnect with the golden age of the late nineteenth century—as suggested by restoration of the "z" to the venerable name of Rauzan—then the mission has been accomplished.

What is astounding is that the man in charge today, John Kolasa, readily admits to being an outsider. Long a teacher of French and graphic arts, this Francophile English humanist "fell into wine by chance." A succession of lucky encounters, sudden infatuations, and rational enthusiasms encouraged him to embark on the task of learning about this mysterious vocation. The ten years Kolasa spent with Jannoueix, an eminent firm of wine dealers, did the rest. His next stop was the holy of holies, Château Latour.

Why did he leave Latour? Because it's always better to be a big fish in a little pond than a little fish in a big one, and because when the owners of the Chanel corporation sought him out they found just the right words to persuade him. In essence: "To each his own. We're in New York, you'll be in Margaux. Tell us what you need, and we'll let you have it. Then all you have to do is get on with it!" Worse hands have been dealt, and our self-taught man didn't have to be asked twice to pick up the cards. He now manages the estate with prudent care. "Each new millesime is like a child you have to bring up," he notes with feeling. "One year it'll be a sturdy

kid, a future rugby player. Fine. The next, it'll be a frailer one, but with artistic leanings. Well, that's fine, too!"

Visitors to Rauzan-Ségla all report the same impression: the people here know how to enjoy nature's bounty. The full-time manager, as well as the vineyard workers who don't mind taking a turn waiting at table in the dining room, all cultivate this ancestral appreciation for the good life, for the gifts offered by the land. Kolasa's English accent is soon forgotten as he expresses the most French of all Gallic imperatives: the importance of living well. "When I assemble a wine," he concludes, "it's always for the purpose of stimulating pleasure and conviviality. Our goal is not to win tasting competitions or to produce bottles of wine that someday will be collectors' items. We do make good bottles of wine, but we always bear in mind that their destiny is to be uncorked and shared among friends."

When all is said and done, does anything else really count?

Glimpsed from afar or admired at leisure, these buildings exhibit a kind of English charm.

CHÂTEAU
RAUZAN-GASSIES

Margaux

The year is 1661. Louis XIV, finally rid of the troublesome Cardinal Richelieu, can begin to reign without interference. Hundreds of miles away in the Médoc region, one of the first great winegrowers, Pierre des Mesures de Rauzan—a man whose name is still revered on the banks of the Gironde—is starting his own dynasty. In 1661, he purchased the vineyards belonging to the noble house of Gassies. Although the vineyards were originally mentioned in the first thirty years of the sixteenth century as belonging to a certain M. Gaillard de Tarde, by the 1660s they were neglected and in poor shape. Pierre des Mesures de Rauzan can certainly claim the distinction of founding the first vineyard worthy of the Bordeaux reputation. Years later, he left his mark on the region again, leasing the châteaux of Margaux and La Tour and founding the Pichon *cru* in Pauillac. The Bordeaux region certainly owes him a great deal.

Pierre de Rauzan's descendants remained in control of their heritage for a period spanning a little over a century, to the last years of the reign of Louis XV. In 1766, however, they were forced to give up part of their lands. The Baroness de Ségla gave her name to part of the estate—the one on which the delightful house stands—while the other part kept the old name. The two parts of the estate were thus known as Rauzan-Ségla and Rauzan-Gassies. In the 1855 classification, both were classed Second Growth *crus*. The then owner was a certain Monsieur Viguerie. The estate changed hands several times over the next few decades.

The Rauzan-Gassies estate was purchased at the end of World War II by the Quié family, who also own Château Croizet-Bages just outside Pauillac. After some years, Paul Quié handed the running of the estate over to his son Jean-Michel. Both have made respect for the old ways and—for the outstanding qualities of the *terroir*—their hallmark. They have made the best of the remarkable qualities of the *terroir*, laying out a large number of small plots along a fossil riverbed of the Gironde. The soil varies from deep gravel to gravelly sand. Nearly all the soil types characteristic of the Médoc are represented.

Bearing eloquent witness to the estate's past, the cellar is a sacred spot where time seems to have stopped.
Shown here, a few bottles that have been slumbering since 1983—an excellent year.

Many of the château's clients are British, a reminder of the days when M. de Rauzan himself regularly traveled to London to sell his wares. Now the British are not best known for their adventurous tastes in wine, which may account for the estate's voluntarily traditionalist approach to wine and winemaking. True, when you visit the fermentation cellar, a stainless steel vat with a capacity of some hundred and five thousand gallons (four thousand hectoliters) stands alongside the rows of old-fashioned aging casks. But that should not be taken as an indication that Jean-Michel Quié, his head of winemaking Jean-Louis Camp, and their team are ready to turn their backs on methods tried and tested for generations, which have always stood both Rauzan-Gassies and Croizet-Bages in good stead. Such old-fashioned methods have earned both estates a solid reputation. The only thing that would make Jean-Michel change his mind would be if the quality of the wine were to suffer. But there seems to be no chance of that happening for the moment. Countless tastings, both in France and abroad, have confirmed the excellent quality and reputation of this superb wine, appreciated by winelovers for its power tempered by great finesse, and the remarkable way it brings out the best qualities of a highly complex *terroir*. The Rauzan-Gassies label, featuring the family's winged coat of arms, is symbolic of the way this wine has soared away from its past difficulties to reach its current heights.

The entrance to the cellars (left), vying with that of the other Rauzan, is designed—like the courtyard and buildings (above, right)—with unadorned simplicity. The attractions of this deuxième grand cru *clearly lie elsewhere. In 1959 the "wings of Gassies" (above, left) were already visible above the medallion.*

CHÂTEAU
LÉOVILLE-POYFERRÉ

Saint-Julien

One cannot approach this estate with a clear mind before first explaining why there are so many different Léovilles. Our explanation begins in the eighteenth century, when Alexandre de Gascq, lord of Léoville, willed the largest winegrowing estate in the Médoc jointly to his four direct heirs. Because one of them, the Marquis de Las Cases, had emigrated, his share defaulted to the state and—after a number of sales and resales—was ultimately acquired by the Barton family. It then became Léoville Barton. With the exception of the Great Court, which remained under joint ownership, the remaining three shares of the property were split in 1840 between the eldest heir, the famous author of the *Mémorial* of St. Helena, who founded Léoville Las Cases, and his sister Jeanne. When Jeanne married the Baron de Poyferré, her share of the property was renamed Léoville-Poyferré.

The Cuvelier family, proud possessors of all the virtues generally associated with people from the north of France, assumed control of Léoville-Poyferré at the conclusion of World War I. In 1979, after six decades, Didier Cuvelier was the first member of the family to take over the helm This exemplar of discipline and foresight immediately set about modernizing his property. He began with the vineyard, which had been reduced to half its original area. At first, all parcels of land in the vineyard were replanted; later, the understock on certain parcels was uprooted and replanted.

During the French economic boom of the 1980s, the estate's new master—a builder by nature as well as by necessity—embarked on a broad range of renovation projects. The finished structures are notable for an aesthetic that combines the use of modern materials with a respect for traditional forms. One example is the new storage cellar, started in 1990 and completed in 1991: with its glass wall and monumental sliding panels, it is considered the jewel of the refurbished Léoville-Poyferré. The winery was completely renovated between 1993 and 1994, and thus boasts cutting-edge winemaking technology.

Inverted checkerboard paving adds a unique elegance
to the estate's spacious fermenting room.

The initial phase of work on the cellars and wineries was completed in 1996, endowing the Poyferré "crew" with efficient and up-to-date tools. This mitigated the effects of the 1840 succession, which forces them to share the château with the Las Cases "crew" and places the Great Court itself under the annoying constraint of joint ownership. The Poyferré "crew" must cross the Route des Vins in order to reach the winery located on the château side, where it forms a little enclave on Las Cases "crew" territory. New architectural projects that are more ambitious than any previously envisioned at Léoville-Poyferré are currently under study and, if implemented, should provide the château with a reception area worthy of its rank.

But Didier Cuvelier is a philosophical man with a sure sense of his priorities. First, he has not lost sight of the true foundation on which the stability of the family property rests. "I never forget that being wine dealers is what enabled us to maintain control of the châteaux in times of economic crisis," he points out. "Marketing is crucial to us and is integral to our overall strategy." Second, in reference to a different aspect of the same subject, he refuses to be lured by the attractions of distant foreign markets at the expense of a more traditional clientele. He explains, "We never want to lose sight of the French market. And this means, among other things, that we can't raise prices indefinitely. Of course we can and do raise our prices from time to time, but we can't let them go through the roof." Wise words, indeed, from the man who concludes, "You can't make a tree grow as high as the sky."

Standing in his elegant, very Art Deco-style office with its yellow walls and doors of exotic wood, Didier Cuvelier frowns and reflects. What new projects are even now germinating behind his furrowed brow? We can be sure of one thing, in any case: before they are adopted, they will be carefully weighed on the scales of reason and moderation. Two virtues of the North, of course, both of them salutary for those who hope to survive over the long term.

Major renovations have been executed over the past twenty-five years, from the monumental entrance to the storage cellars (above, right), to the barrel vault of this modular cellar (left).

CHÂTEAU
LÉOVILLE BARTON

Saint-Julien

The legendary Hugh Barton, who already managed the family wine business in Bordeaux at the time of the Revolution, did not escape the fatal impact of the "terror," and in October 1973, he was arrested with his wife, stripped of his possessions, and threatened with the guillotine! By good fortune, he escaped and returned to his native Ireland. When the storm had passed, he returned to the Médoc and took advantage of the considerable changes in ownership of land in France at that era, buying Château Langoa and a part of Léoville in 1826.

The portion of the vineyard which became Léoville Barton, was at that time devoid of any building and was to remain so. Nonetheless, it is the great wine of Léoville that the sacred classification chose to be included among the second growths, leaving its big brother to take its place among the thirds. Awkward neighbors—not only the house belongs to Langoa, but the cellars too. One might therefore say that Léoville consists of a vineyard only. The greater part consists of a mound with ideal exposition. The soil is gravel on a sub-soil of clay and limestone.

As for the wine itself—how can one describe "the immediate and sensual seduction of this deep color, of this bouquet both rich and concentrated which is confirmed on the palate, this soft velvety flavor which lingers on thanks to a good tannic structure, firm but balanced," to quote the descriptions, always rather standard, of the oenologist. If there exist wines which are self-sufficient and need no addition, then this wine most certainly belongs to that category.

There is in this noble beverage of Léoville Barton much more than a trace of the characters so marked of those who, since Hugh in the past up to Anthony of today, have contributed the best of themselves. In this way somewhere deep in each bottle of Léoville Barton there lies hidden something of the personality of these Irishmen who for so many generations have settled with such success on the banks of the Gironde.

Hugh Barton (1766–1854), fourth son of William, was undoubtedly the most prominent member of the family. After the French Revolution, it is he who acquired Langoa (to be admired on the following double page) and then part of Léoville.

CHÂTEAU
DURFORT-VIVENS

Margaux

Shortly before the French Revolution, and hence long before wines were given the official rankings we know today, the illustrious Thomas Jefferson took a tour of the Médoc region and thought it would be amusing to establish his own listing. He awarded first place to Lafite, Latour, and Margaux—a choice borne out by history—and put Durfort-Vivens next on the list. This was also shrewd. Over two centuries later, any second *grand cru* can definitely take pride in such an honor. Some opinions are like diplomas or military medals: although they add nothing to inherent merit, they do provide it with tangible recognition.

Durfort-Vivens has not escaped the vicissitudes of history and has thus several times changed owners during the twentieth century. The Lurtons were shareholders of Château Margaux when it acquired Durfort in 1937. They were shareholders no longer when they resold it in 1962 to . . . Lucien Lurton. Later, Château Margaux combined with Brane-Catenac—there are far worse fates for a great vintage!

In 1992, the task of putting the estate back on its own feet fell to one of Lucien Lurton's sons, Gonzague. In 1995, Gonzague Lurton began by endowing the estate with efficient equipment. This required a substantial investment in order to give Durfort-Vivens the means to achieve its high goals. The investment was made; a stunning paradox is the artful combination of cutting-edge technology with more traditional materials such as the wood used for roof-beams and casks, highlighting the infinite richness of a gleaming floor.

There are some who would have rested on their laurels after this initial success, but Gonzague Lurton is not one of them. In his view, this was just the beginning. What he aimed for was to forge new and solid links with the estate's pre-eminent reputation, and he succeeded in a very short time. A glance at the opinions of contemporary wine critics—both French and international—provides convincing proof that Durfort-Vivens again occupies the lofty position it had held for two centuries.

The freshly scrubbed paving in the fermenting room reflects vats
made of two different materials: wood and stainless steel.

Gonzague Lurton and his team best efforts go into the vineyard itself, of course. Their guiding principle is obvious: to produce a great wine reflecting as faithfully as possible the soil in which the grapes are grown. A wine that could not be made anywhere else, a wine from this specific place and no other. In fact, when you stop to think about it, what better way could there be of eliminating competition from the so-called "New World" wines? In this context, the very term "New World" is absurd. Here in the Old World— when the living raw materials of grape and soil are respected, when the vibrant harmony between them, which from afar seems almost supernatural, is achieved—then the challenge is easily met.

In the same spirit, it is important to banish all methods and processes, from pruning to bottling, that don't include the gentle and inimitable touch of the human hand. Gonzague Lurton and his team work on the assumption that there is no product more human than this one, and they are right. At Durfort-Vivens, methods, tools, and even yields are adapted to the measure of man—the alpha and omega of all that occurs between the estate's walls. The rest is an intoxication of the spirit. For the best of reasons, some of the fermenting rooms and cellars are brand-new; but, even so, they are already imbued with that delicate scent of wine which, according to the foremost of our humanists, is "O! how much more sweet, joyous, and reverent, how much more celestial and delicious!"

The corner building overlooking the "Route des Vins" (facing page), contains an ancient cooper's workshop (right, center). Behind it are new buildings housing the cellars (right, top and bottom).

CHÂTEAU
GRUAUD LAROSE

Saint-Julien

From the top of the impressive square tower, where a banner in the estate's colors flutters gaily in the breeze, you can see for miles over the surrounding countryside. The estate itself, in the heart of the Saint-Julien *appellation*, covers almost three hundred acres (more than a hundred and twenty hectares), two hundred of which are planted with vines. From the top of the tower, you can make out the neat edges of the plots, planted around the château, and the anti-hail system—a sonic cannon which every now and then booms out over the vines. Not far off are the outbuildings, vast and impersonal, a superb neoclassic house, built in 1875 in imitation of the eighteenth-century style, and the neat gardens with their pretty rosebeds—a witty reference to the name of the estate. Gruaud Larose certainly looks the picture of the ideal winegrowing estate.

The estate was founded by a certain Monsieur Gruaud, but it was his nephew, Monsieur Larose, who first earned it its fine reputation. In the nineteenth century, the estate was split into two, with a château on each half—Château Gruaud Larose Sarget and Château Gruaud Larose Faure. The two halves were reunited in 1935 when they were bought by the Cordier family. The estate passed into the hands of the industrial giant Alcatel-Alsthom in September 1993. Just over three years later, Pierre Suard, the group's managing director at the time, decided it was rather an expensive luxury and sold it off, after having spent lavishly on bringing all the equipment up to date and hiring the finest specialists to work on the estate, including the well-known architect Philippe Mazières.

Gruaud Larose, "the wine of kings, the king of wines," was bought by the family-run wine merchants Bernard Taillan Vins in spring 1997. They appointed Jean Merlaut managing director of the estate. He is a local man, Médoc born and bred, who always knew his destiny was to work in one of the great vineyards. It is rather humbling to talk to such a man who measures time and progress in half-centuries and who has a depth of knowledge, built up over generations, at his fingertips. He has an instinctive feel for

This vast underground cellar with its canopy
of low vaulting recalls ancient crypts.

making the best of the weather and adapting to the demands of the marketplace. He explains, "In this region, first we cut and sold wood. Then we planted grain to sell, which rebalanced the soil so we could plant vines. You see, it's in our nature to see the long-term picture and to think in terms of cycles that can last for decades."

Georges Pauli, the estate's head technician oenologist (expert), originally hired by the Cordier family, agrees with Jean Merlaut when it comes to discussing the soil. He nods in agreement as Jean says, "The *terroir* is anything but inert. What we do to it can make it sterile or more fertile. It is a living being, and it needs looking after long-term." Jean is gentle, self-effacing, and discreet. He tells me, "I'd hate it if people started saying, 'you can tell this is one of Jean Merlaut's wines.' I have to say, for me, the secret of good winemaking is to step back and let the grapes do the talking." He adds as an afterthought, "That's why we put such a lot of work into the vines."

As we tour the fermentation cellar, Jean waves cheerily to the employees hard at work. He prefers using concrete vats which, as well as being chemically inert and maintaining a stable temperature, have corners which help the wine mix well as it ferments by creating currents. In the elegant, low-ceilinged cellar, with its rows of casks, he explains where the oak used to make the casks comes from. "You could say that wood has its own *terroir*, just like wine. The quality of the soil the tree grew in definitely has an effect on the taste of the wine. We're working on that side of things at the moment."

But like so many other estate managers, Jean Merlaut is convinced that the most important factor is the human touch. "The wine trade is all about transmitting your passion to your team first of all, and then to the customers. That's why we've decided to implement a new system which takes into account the personal motivation of each of our employees, sharing out more responsibility. Of course, the *terroir* is where it all begins. But by far the most important factor is the time and effort put in by the men who make the wine. The quality of the finished product is the direct outcome of how well they do their work."

Flanked by its watchtower, the neo-Louis XVI manor house (facing page) contains elegant salons in various styles (right, top). The impressive size of the cellars and buildings reflects the scope of the estate's operations (right, center and bottom).

CHÂTEAU
LASCOMBES

Margaux

L ascombes straddling two ages, two eras. Is it too late to praise the rich history of an estate that was once exceptional and then declined somewhat, or too soon to evoke the incredible efforts currently undertaken to restore its rightful luster to this gem of the Bordeaux region? The one thing we can say with certainty is that Lascombes is in a phase of renewal, of strength for once again attaining the first rank.

Because it is located in one of the best parcels of the Margaux *appellation*, this estate has produced numerous admirable vintages in the years since it was first created by the lord of Lascombes in the seventeenth century. "Its wines are reputed to be of such superior quality that they rival those of Château Margaux," reports a wine-trade publication in its 1938 issue. It is thus not surprising to find Lascombes listed among the brilliant *seconds crus* of the original 1855 rankings. The actual château, still shown on the wine's labels, was built twelve years later under the direction of a Bordeaux lawyer, Chaix d'Est Ange.

Over time, the Château has succeeded in preserving its place among the first rank of Médoc estates. This rank, this status, and this reputation were bound to interest a man such as Alexis Lichine. It did not take long for the great man to persuade a number of wealthy American friends—including David Rockefeller—to invest in its acquisition. This is how the great wine was revived and became a "must-have" in the United States, where its reputation reached a high point in the 1950s and an even higher one in the 1960s. A decline began in 1971: the new owner, British brewer Bass-Charrington, experienced problems in understanding the subtleties of winemaking. Lascombes gradually succumbed to the fatal cult of high yield and, as a result, inevitably declined over the succeeding years. An imposing fermenting room containing thirty heat-regulated vats was installed in 1986 and became a sort of wine-country tourist attraction. But this was not enough.

In April 2001 this sleeping beauty was acquired by an American investment fund, Colony Capital. Gigantic

Drenched in a luminously futuristic atmosphere,
this aging cellar can be seen as the archetype of modern winery buildings.

renovation projects were initiated both in the 207-acre (84-hectare) vineyard, which was completely overhauled, and in the winery, where ultramodern buildings—no doubt the most spectacular in the region—rose from the ground in just a few months. New energy was infused into the property under the direction of oenologist Michel Rolland, who informed the press, "I have no intention of abandoning the qualities typical of Margaux wines. What I want to do is to make a Margaux, a truly great one." The means are there, and almost limitless, but the results are slow to arrive . . . Patience!

No one would deny that this patience is one of the new team's outstanding virtues, not to mention its rigor and innovative spirit. Drawing on a tradition going back at least three hundred years, and also on the remarkable progress made thanks to recent investments, Sébastien Bazin, president, Dominique Befve, managing director, and Delphine Barboux, quality coordinator, have swiftly regained, for their annual production of 250,000 bottles, their wine's rightful rank in the appellation. The experts recognize this, as does the trade press, which since 2001 has hailed the return of Lascombes to the summits, to the strength and body of a great Margaux.

Covered with virginia creeper like an old presbytery, the beautiful house (facing page) contains several pretty drawing rooms (left, center). The intricate ironwork of the front gate (left, bottom) can also be found on the label of this great wine (left, top); here a bottle of 1952 from the Saint des Saints is presented.

CHÂTEAU
BRANE-CANTENAC

Margaux

nder the July Monarchy, Baron Hector de Brane was one of the most dynamic estate owners in the Médoc. There was even a local saying, referring to the promise of flowering vines in spring, "The baron is racking his wine." Better still—or more emphatically, in any case—the baron's fellow vintners dubbed him the "Napoleon of the Vines." That such a man could, in July 1833, voluntarily divest himself of a property like Mouton—the future Mouton Rothschild—in order to devote himself more fully to his Gorce (also spelled "Gorse") estate gives some idea of the latter property's contemporary reputation. Five years later, the baron informed wine critics that, "The name of Gorce is justifiably respected in Bordeaux and abroad, but that of Brane no less so. In any case, rightly or wrongly, through self-indulgence or pride, I believe in my name and I would like, with your help, to phase out the name Gorce and replace it with Brane-Cantenac."

This is the story behind one of the most prestigious names appearing in the 1855 rankings, one placed unanimously among the *seconds crus*. Acquired by the Berger family toward the end of the Second Empire, the estate was continually enlarged and improved. The very best was made of this exceptional soil, of this admirable mound of local gravel from the Garonne river. In the beginning of the following century, prices for the estate's wines reached the apex of the great Bordeaux-wine hierarchy.

Today, the estate's current owner correctly underscores the role played by World War I in the fate of ancient wine-growing estates. Numerous properties changed hands in the aftermath of the 1919 victory, and Brane-Cantenac was one of them. Léonce Récapet and his son-in-law François Lurton, who purchased the estate in 1922, were at the time major shareholders in Château Margaux, and several of the vineyards included in this Bordeaux gem were then attached to Brane-Cantenac.

Lucien Lurton inherited the property in 1956, the dire year of the great freeze. As so often happens, however, this apparent calamity turned out to be a blessing in disguise,

It would take an entire book to describe the extraordinary surge of renewal and modernization experienced by this vineyard since the beginning of the 1980s. The estate's new offices provide one eloquent example.

providing the entire Médoc region with a much-needed chance to start over from scratch. Lucien Lurton naturally chose Brane-Cantenac as the flagship of an armada composed of Durfort-Vivens, Desmirail, etc. He and his brother André were perfect examples of the entrepreneurial businessmen to whom France owed *Les Trente Glorieuses*, or thirty years of dramatic economic recovery. But this is far from the whole story. According to Lucien Lurton's son Henri, director of the estate since 1992, inheriting joint ownership of Brane-Cantenac in the mid-1950s was no picnic.

Today, the single aspect of the estate of keenest interest to Henri Lurton is the vineyard itself. Extensive soil analyses provide detailed descriptions of each parcel of land so they can be exploited with maximum effect. Although the vinification methods at Brane-Cantenac are highly innovative, they take second place to care of the vines themselves. In the current management team's view, technology should be subservient to the soil. "Of course we must try to surpass ourselves in creating the best possible product," states Henri

Lurton unambiguously, "but everything we do is actually focused on the soil that provides the raw material."

It is thus hardly surprising that Brane-Cantenac can be counted today among the great wines most elegantly expressing the elegant properties—particularly the aromatic ones—of the Margaux *appellation*. As long as the estate's owners continue to show total respect for the perfect health of their soil, and the unique assets it confers on their nectar, they will indeed continue to be worthy of the decision taken in the distant past by the "Napoleon of the Vines."

Here, the photographer has succeeded in capturing the elusive magic pervading this fine cask cellar, in which the shadows lift their heavy veil only under the rays of indirect light (left). The rest is less mysterious, as indicated by these functional buildings with the pretty stone ties (above, left), and the charterhouse itself, which stands out curiously among its surroundings (above, right).

CHÂTEAU
PICHON-LONGUEVILLE

Pauillac

In the mid-nineteenth century, when the Baron de Longueville divided his estate among his sons and daughters, the share of the vineyard inherited by his two sons covered two-fifths of the total area—or the approximate area of the Pichon-Longueville vineyard today. For over a century, the wines produced on this land faithfully reflected their well-earned second *grand cru* ranking.

Over a century later, however, Pichon-Longueville was faltering in the race against its "rival sister" Pichon Longueville Comtesse de Lalande. By the early 1980s the mighty ship was adrift and in desperate need of someone to mend its hull and refit it from stem to stern. In other words, an investor willing to restore its vanished luster. The AXA group saved the day, and Pichon-Longueville became the flagship of this insurance giant's armada, following a course charted by Jean-Michel Cazes.

Any change in estate management inevitably affects the land as well as the buildings. The time had come for Pichon-Longueville to make a fresh start, but it was also important to preserve the treasures inherited from the past. In 1986 plans for a new winery were selected on the basis of an architectural competition supervised by the Centre National Georges Pompidou, then represented by Jean Dethier.

The winners' vision was both impressive and simple. Their plan combined architectural daring with profound respect for a heritage that had finally come into its own. The château was restored, but otherwise left basically unchanged. No one wanted to recut this period gem, which was merely endowed with an ultracontemporary setting designed to enhance it without overwhelming it.

The result is a partially sunken horizontal pattern of walls with vanishing lines of perspective inspired by ancient Egypt, and ornamental pools worthy of a festival *Magic Flute*—the whole serving as an ideal setting for the resurrected château. The walls, built in the style of early Egyptian tombs, are cleverly used to conceal exits and entrances, the winery, storage areas, and of course the circular fermenting

The waters of the square pool in the center of the courtyard
reflect the façade's Renaissance architecture.

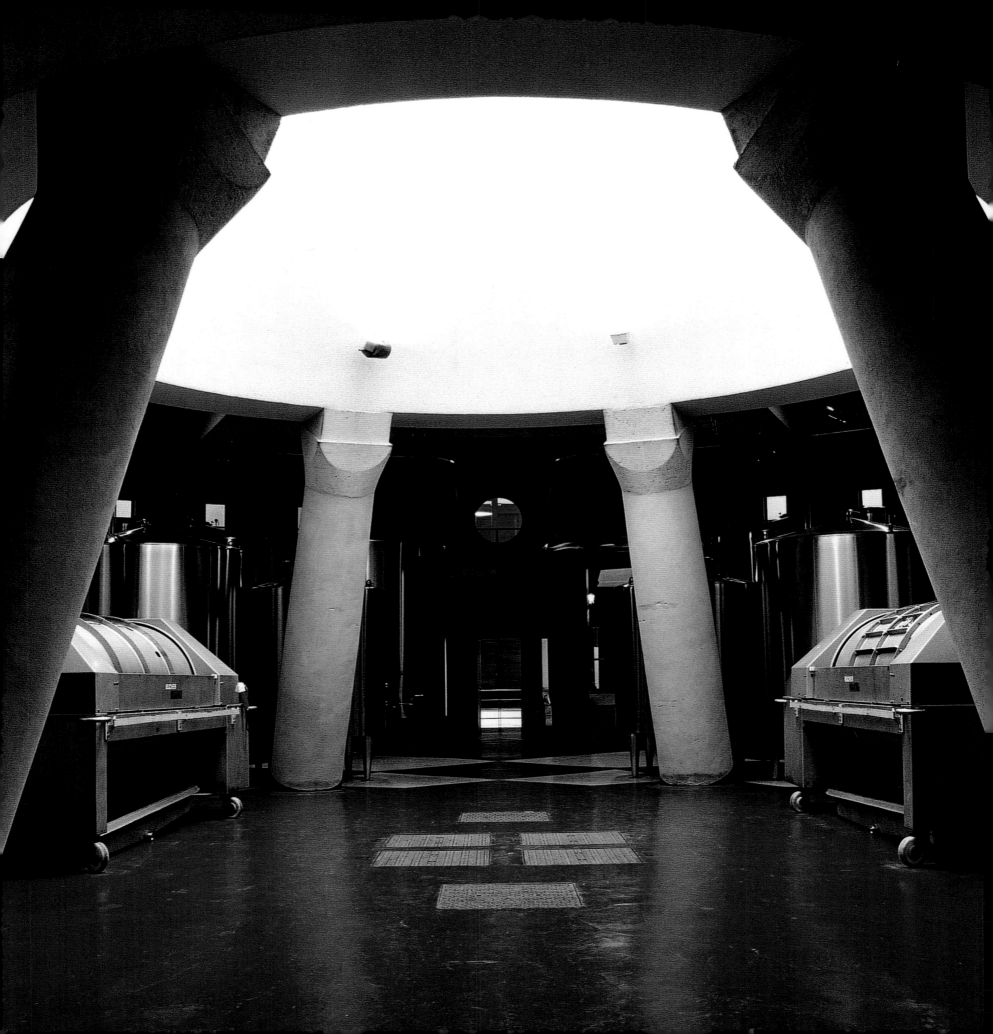

room with its rows of columns—a flattering imitation of the same installation at Mouton Rothschild, and also an adroit solution to certain technical problems.

The wild enthusiasm of this imposing décor's supporters is matched by the fierce criticism of its detractors—but never mind. The most positive thing about it is the discretion with which its designers, the Franco-American team of Jean de Gastines and Patrick Dillon, have integrated it with the rest of the site.

Their philosophy is perfectly in tune with that of the estate's current managing director, Christian Seely. A thoughtful and judicious man, Seely is fully conscious that he is merely the temporary guardian of a heritage "which existed long before we did and will continue to exist long after we are gone," and accepts the fact that he plays a supporting role compared to the real hero of the drama: the soil. As Seely tirelessly repeats, "Our task is to help the soil express itself as fully as possible, and to protect it from harm."

This ethics of respect is obvious everywhere on the estate, in every one of its operations. Respect for the environment, respect for the land and its fruits, respect for the natural rhythms of time. The proud Pichon-Longueville team has won its ISO 14001 quality certification, the first estate in the region to do so. They see this as a reward less for hard work and discipline than for the attentive care unstintingly given to a living vineyard—a vineyard that is loved, tended, and cherished.

The famous rotunda fermenting room (facing page)
and a number of borrowings from the Egyptian style (right)
are the work of the audacious Dillon-de Gastine duo.

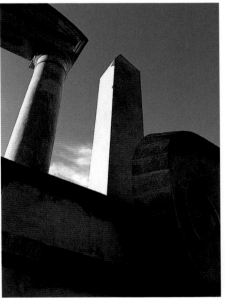

CHÂTEAU
PICHON LONGUEVILLE
COMTESSE DE LALANDE

Pauillac

In the mostly male-dominated world of great Bordeaux wines, this estate adds the touch of femininity needed to restore the balance. Eve rather than Adam is a pervasive presence here, in a lovely garden filled with fragrant plants (laurels, roses, cypresses), and in a beautifully designed manor house, inspired by the Lalande family's Bordeaux town house. In its two charming salons—one white, the other pink—a floral décor is accented by romantic paintings dashed off in a bygone age by a talented ancestor who alternated stormy landscapes with serene family portraits. Women have always been responsible for the production of this second *cru classé* wine, and it comes as no surprise to learn that they did it in their own unique way.

The first of these women was the daughter of Pierre de Rauzan, and it was she who—through her marriage to a certain Jacques de Pichon in 1694—gave the estate its name. However, we should not accord more importance to this gentlewoman than she deserves. The true latter-day founder of the estate was indeed a man: Baron Joseph, whose high standards ensured the domain's quality and endurance. Baron Joseph died in 1850, at the age of one hundred, after having divided the property among his children: two-fifths for his two sons, three-fifths for his three daughters. The youngest daughter, Virginie, turned out to be the most energetic. When she married, she became the Comtesse de Lalande, eventually acquiring her sisters' shares of the estate and creating her own fiefdom separate from that of the other Pichon—the baron.

The indomitable Comtesse de Lalande! The new estate owed its enviable position in the 1855 rankings to her tireless industry and firm hand. From 1850 until 1882 she succeeded in raising her estate to the summits of excellence. As she herself put it, somewhat grandiloquently, "After I am gone, I want an unforgettable wine to remain." And in fact, this woman who reigned as a sort of local Queen Victoria marked the château with an indelible imprint that was hers and hers alone—so much so that no one else ever considered changing so much as a single piece of furniture.

Drawing its inspiration from the Lalande town house in Bordeaux,
the château boasts a stunning central tower-staircase.

Pichon Longueville Comtesse de Lalande was handed down from generation to generation, from aunt to niece, until the economic crisis of the 1920s, when the vineyard was acquired by the brothers Miailhe. Does this mean the château reverted "to the males"? Not for long, in any case. Today, responsibility again resides in a woman, the enterprising and dynamic May-Eliane de Lencquesaing. Her father was one of the purchasers in 1925, and she has been responsible for managing the estate since 1978. The Miailhe heiress is a remarkable and attractive woman. She relentlessly defends the regimental colors of her estate with all the energy proper to the wife of a military man. "You know the view from the main terrace?" she asks. As her little King Charles spaniel barks exuberantly, she points out the spots where major investments have been made over the past twenty years.

She has friends all over the world, and they make frequent visits, which she returns. Whether sallying forth to conquer the natives of New Orleans and Hong Kong, or hosting dinners for guests from Korea and the Philippines, this cheerful, bilingual woman, a worthy heiress of the late Comtesse, relishes her exhausting life as an ambassador. She has written a short story on her favorite subject, entitled *Je suis vivant, dit le Vin* ("I'm Alive, Says the Wine") and, with her nephew Gildas d'Ollone, seeks for ways to teach the world how it is that wine brings us closer to God. Meanwhile, she also organizes impressive exhibitions of contemporary glass in the conservatory she founded, which—in an ideal setting—is dedicated to the art of glassware over the ages. Glass, and the wine it holds: daring, translucence, fragility.

A highly feminine charm imbues the salons, the glassware collection, and even the vast Latour terrace (right).
The stunning piece (facing page) entitled Athamas *was created by Jean Cocteau for Daum.*

CHÂTEAU
DUCRU-BEAUCAILLOU

Saint-Julien

The byword here is "equilibrium." Purity, rigor, and surpassing effort are, of course, claimed in the brochures; but these are nothing compared with the supreme—"inherent," one is tempted to say—tension establishing perfect balance. It is true, of course, that the site lends itself in a curious way to this very quality. The estate is located midway between the village of Beychevelle and the Gironde riverbed; lying peacefully under the passing clouds, it dominates the alluvial land below from a hillock of Garonne gravel infinitely favorable to the growth of perfect grapes.

The terrace is one of the gems of the Bordeaux region, prized for the magical view it offers from its slight elevation over the river, and for its position adjacent to the Saint-Julien plateau. Over the treacherous marshes, shifting blue reflections from the distant river flowing behind ancient and rare trees paint the horizon with the heart-stopping tones that constitute the true beauty of all estuary landscapes.

Ducru-Beaucaillou. The name may seem bizarre, but it has its own logic. The "*beaux cailloux*" are the smooth, round, flat, unusually large pebbles that lie beneath the mature (over forty years in age) and numerous (four thousand per acre or ten thousand per hectare) roots of the vineyard. The most transparent of these pebbles are dubbed "roadmen's sugar cubes" by the people of the Périgord. Ducru is the name of the family that in the period of the French Directory acquired an estate reputed to be nothing but arid, stony ground. Nevertheless, the Ducrus decided to plant a vineyard on it. Since then, all of their successors have worked hard to extract from the depths of this inhospitable soil the quintessence of a great Médoc wine. And they have succeeded, approaching an archetypal level of quality and earning a reputation as the "most accomplished of all Bordeaux wines." The famed Johnston wine dealers have been unsparing in their efforts and, if this great *second cru* is both mellow and powerful, full-bodied and rich—but above all vigorous—this is due primarily to their expertise.

The Johnstons were also responsible for the restoration of two symmetrical pavilions in the form of square romantic towers on either side of the elegant charterhouse. These are called Victorian, and are certainly reminiscent of that era's

The large central salon has preserved its fine nineteenth-century décor,
featuring woodwork and tapestry.

pleasure follies. The partly subterranean new winery beneath a steep grassy ramp connected by architect Alain Triaud to the base of the house offers a streamlined counterpoint to these more grandiloquent vestiges of a golden age. Bruno Borie, the contemporary heir to all of this, exhibits a stoicism no doubt inevitable in a fourth-generation owner. Although he has nothing to prove, he's keenly aware that no one will cut him any slack—and he accepts it. He's been at the helm, personally, for only a short time, and is determined to add a few stones of his own to the edifice—calmly, imperturbably, with the equanimity of a man who knows he's well armed for the battles ahead, and is prepared to face them squarely.

There is something vaguely British in the witty remarks of this master of understatement. He admires the English for their past ability to assimilate all the refinements of the planet, and declares somewhat ruefully that "great wines never taste better than at a club on Pall Mall." His own work ethic reflects the fact that he has obviously studied the lessons of Albion and asks nothing better for his own nectar than to win a place for it in a long and vibrant chain of excellence and tradition. "Nature's rhythms teach us patience," he says, "and in the Médoc we know how to work for coming generations. I'm nearing retirement, but I can still feel excitement at the idea of planting a vine that will not bear its succulent fruit for another ten or fifteen years."

Bruno Borie and his team are working for future generations, and they see themselves as "midwives" at the birth of a potential representing the promise of everything they believe in. "The quality ranked in 1855," he claims, "was simply a potential for excellence. It's up to us to realize that potential." An admirable philosophy, to be sure, and one that—through the implementation of a subtle equilibrium—consists in giving concrete form to an ideal.

The wind rustles in the trees. Yes, it is true that, when they come here, people weary of being bombarded with the stubborn tendency of *grand cru* wines to imitate each other in their endless internecine battles, will be relieved to note that true worth is often found in the middle rather than at the top; and that perfection, if it exists, is attained only through balance and moderation—the prerequisites of harmony.

The fermenting vat and cellars form part of a daring architecture (right, bottom) providing an attractive contrast to the Victorian-style buildings (right, top).

CHÂTEAU
COS D'ESTOURNEL

Saint-Estèphe

"When you get to the elephant, the gate will open automatically." These instructions, heard in the depths of the Médoc region, but more like something out of the *Arabian Nights*, immediately plunge visitors into the exotic atmosphere of an Indian bazaar. A tall, marvelously carved wooden panel from Zanzibar, rows of palm trees, a few *azulejos* in an exuberant colonial style, and especially the château's pagoda roof, all contribute to creating a setting as alluring as it is unexpected in these climes. The décor calls for clear blue skies, but overcast weather isn't bad either: it affords added substance and perhaps even greater impact to the whole. No doubt about it: Cos d'Estournel is an oriental folly, but a folly on the grand scale. As Stendhal noted in passing, "It is highly agreeable and in something of the Chinese style."

Biarnez, bard of the Médoc, wrote these lines in its honor:
On these slopes its minarets stand tall,
Oriental façades rise at heaven's beckoning call,
Proud to be the superb delight of which nabobs tell,
This is Cos d'Estournel.

The man primarily responsible for this burst of local color lived under the July Monarchy. Louis-Gaspard d'Estournel was not only a consummate dandy and past master in the art of dazzling, he also cultivated a taste for travel and a love of foreign shores. The structure he built on the gentle promontory facing Lafite did not perhaps enjoy universal approval at first; today, however, it has made the estate famous well beyond the confines of its region.

It should be pointed out that the Prats, owners of the estate since World War I, are just as attuned to aesthetic considerations as their illustrious predecessor. The promotional materials designed for tourists are a perfect example of this. A red, gilt-embossed, imitation-leather folder with accordion sides and moiré pockets holds an elegant leaflet describing the copperplate engraving on the château's labels, giving a short history of the estate illustrated with watercolors, and including sumptuous photographic plates in black-and-white and color, glossy and matte; and—to top it all off—one souvenir notebook filled with portraits of grape pickers, another featuring maharajahs.

A sense of visual esthetics and a taste for detail
are also apparent in the tasting room.

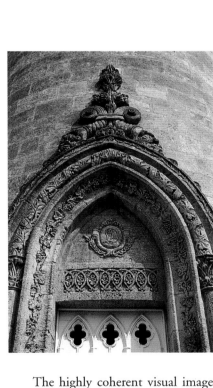

The highly coherent visual image projected by all of this—as by the well-lit wine cellars, filled with rows of pale wooden casks placed against a dark background as if in a museum worthy of the finest exhibitions—is the work of Jean-Marie Prats. This pervasive style, visible even on the souvenir "Cos d'Estournel" silk squares, might almost make one forget the true lord of the manor: a great Saint-Estèphe wine, ranked *Second Cru* in 1855 and once served at the tables of French Emperor Napoleon III, British Queen Victoria, and the Russian Czar. A wine which has been impressing connoisseurs ever since.

Jean-Marie's brother Bruno has labored for decades to maintain and continually improve the quality of this regal, balanced, and harmonious nectar that boasts an unexpected touch of the exotic: it has a note of tannin, but only a faint one, combined with infinitely subtle aromas of fruit, spice, and chocolate. Today, at the dawn of a new millennium, the Prats have finally passed on the torch. But the new owner, Michel Raybien, has kept at the helm a certain Jean-Guillaume . . . Prats. A man who refuses to stray from the path traced by his elders. "Blood will tell," as the saying goes—and so will great vintages that keep faith with themselves. A philosophy perfectly expressed by this estate's motto: *Semper Fidelis*.

A dreamlike vision at the heart of the Saint-Estèphe vineyard. The pagodas (left) anchor the château in an atmosphere of exoticism that also casts its spell over the tower's Manoeline décor (above, left). Even the cask cellar has succumbed to this dizzying theatricality (above, center).

131

CHÂTEAU
MONTROSE

Saint-Estèphe

Where did the name come from? What's that tall metallic mast for? Why are those French-style street-name signs tacked onto the corners of some buildings? Visitors to this estate start asking questions the moment they cross the threshold, and owner Jean-Louis Charmolüe has ready answers for all of them. The name Montrose comes from the heather that once grew on the moors covering these slopes, and its lovely color like the lees of wine. *Se non è vero, è ben trovato*. That mast, like a miniature Eiffel Tower patriotically etched against the sky of Aquitaine, once—back in the evil days of the phylloxera epidemic—supported a windmill connected to a water pump. As for the street signs, Charmolüe is definitely the one to ask, since he's the man who put them there. He wanted to emphasize the resemblance of this model estate—with its alleyways, little open squares, and streets of workshops and houses for the vineyard workers—to a real village. The signs are classic blue with white lettering, the names those of major vintners—and Dumoulin tops the list, of course.

The Dumoulins are the people who purchased the property, during the reign of Louis XVI, from the celebrated Alexandre de Ségur. Under the Restoration they added a fine neoclassic manor house, planted the first grape vines, and began producing wine magnificent enough to be listed in the 1855 rankings as a *second cru classé*. Toward the end of the Second Empire, the Dollfus family from Alsace acquired an estate that was by then more than promising, and they continued to increase its potential significantly. Various financial transactions in the late nineteenth century resulted in the acquisition of the Montrose estate by the Charmolües, who have been guiding its fortunes for over a century.

The name of the patrician Charmolüe family is a venerable one in the annals of Noyons and Compiègne. The family's dedication, discipline, and moderation have not, however, prevented it from embarking on heroic exploits. Jean-Louis is far more than the grandson of the man who founded the Montrose dynasty; his reign will be as hard to follow as Queen Victoria's was. Jean-Louis has governed this

Like a lookout mast facing the northern tip of peninsula and estuary,
the Eiffel-tower-like structure of the old windmill dominates the estate.

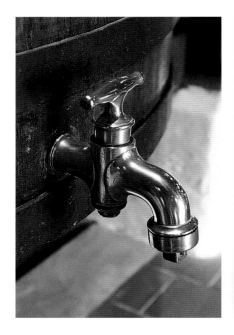  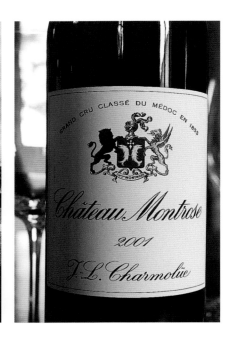 

realm since 1960, and since 1977 he has governed alone. A monarchy exercised in a context of concern for the future, for continuity, but also for change if change is called for.

The vineyard itself—some hundred and sixty-five acres (sixty-six hectares) of land in one continuous piece, with broad, straight paths running through its even rows—features a host of assets: the convenient proximity of the Gironde estuary, for example, protects it almost completely from frost, and the nearby presence of Latour is confirmation of an almost ideal silicon-gravel content in the soil, enhanced by the gentle downward slope of the vineyard toward the river. Here, as at neighboring Latour, the vines are planted north to south for maximum exposure to the sun.

Jean-Louis and Anne-Marie Charmolüe have fond feelings for the past, as demonstrated by the extensive collection of horse-drawn carriages that adds its own note of quaint charm to the scene. But the couple's reverence for the

past has not made them hostile to the innovations of the present. Modern technology is welcomed at Montrose, not scorned. To cite just one example, the new and recently inaugurated winery is visibly one of the estate's most modern features, proof of a conscious desire on the part of its owners to foster continual advance. Taken all in all, it should come as no surprise that the incomparable quality of the great Montrose wines maintains its popularity year after year among the most discriminating connoisseurs, and that even the severest critics rank it at the top of its category.

The Charmolüe family coat of arms appears proudly in the depths of the aging cellar (right) and on the great wine's label (above, right). The mansion, with its miniature peristyle (above, center), has a nobility all of its own.

Château Kirwan

Château d'Issan

Château Lagrange

Château Langoa Barton

Château Giscours

Château Malescot Saint-Exupéry

Château Boyd-Cantenac

Château Cantenac Brown

Château Palmer

Château La Lagune

Château Desmirail

Château Calon Ségur

Château Ferrière

Château Marquis d'Alesme Becker

CHÂTEAU
KIRWAN

Margaux

Nathalie Schÿler's voice takes on a nostalgic note as she recalls the grape harvests when she was a little girl. She describes the scene so well that you might think you were there by her side, listening to the heavy tread of the horses and the laughter of the itinerant grape-pickers from over the border in Spain, gathering up the bunches of grapes that fall off the overflowing pickers' baskets as they head for a quick picnic lunch in the barn where they are spending the summer. That was a good few years ago, when the estate still produced milk in its own dairy, just like the toy dairy for Marie Antoinette in Versailles. Nowadays, the expense of running such a small dairy would make each liter of milk costlier than a bottle of the finest Bordeaux! So the cows have gone to pasture, along with the horses, and nearly all the old traditions have died out. All that remains of the old ways are Nathalie's memories and her steely determination to produce as high-quality a wine as she can.

The Schÿlers have been living in the house on the estate for generations. These days, they do spend the winter months in warmer climes. Time seems to have stood still here. The pretty gardens are kept in meticulous condition, as is the greenhouse, reminiscent of a gentler past when pleasures were enjoyed slowly and to the full—although it was actually built fairly recently. The shaded walk strewn with roses reminded me of the flowery summer hats with delicate veils worn by our grandmothers.

But Kirwan is far from outdated. The estate has invested heavily in all sorts of modern winemaking technology, and while all these investments have been made with the rich lessons of past experience firmly in mind, the estate's managers are now looking ahead to the future to show off the fruits of their work. This does not mean, however, that the current generation has turned its back on all the characteristics that have given past vintages their defining charm. For example, some ten percent of the estate—a relatively high proportion—is still planted with the subtle and unpredictable petit verdot grape variety. "It was something my father, Jean-Henri Schÿler, felt strongly about—you might call it his

The old cellars have been renovated,
and can now accommodate visitors.

personal touch," Nathalie says. "And in fact, some years, it's the petit verdot grapes that give us some of our finest wines."

The Kirwan estate occupies close to ninety acres (thirty-five hectares). Its perimeter has hardly changed since 1855. The highest point of the estate lies at its heart, more than sixty-five feet (twenty meters) above the Cantenac plateau. These parts of the estate benefit from exceptional exposure to the sun. In winemaking, you can't go far wrong with a good *terroir*. The Kirwan *terroir* gives this excellent Third Growth label a grace and well-rounded character that winelovers all over the world appreciate. It is a worthy member of the Margaux *appellation*.

The Schÿler family can be relied upon to sing the praises of their wine, both in France and abroad. It is a long family tradition, stretching back to the early days of the Bordeaux wine merchants set up in 1739 by the Schröder and Schÿler families. Today, you will often hear a babble of foreign languages at their dinner table. The family has particularly strong ties with Denmark. They have welcomed Queen Margrethe II of Denmark as a private guest, and the honorary title of Consul General of Denmark in Bordeaux is handed down from father to son.

The Schÿlers owe much of their reputation to their generosity and hospitality. For a few years now, the estate has been open to tourists or, rather, winelovers eager to explore the secrets of a great Margaux label. The Schÿlers welcome their guests and show them around the well-kept grounds and vineyards with evident delight. Like many great estates, Kirwan takes great pride in putting on as neat and well-ordered an appearance as possible. It is as if there were some mysterious alchemy between the beauty of the grounds and the quality of the wine—as if the good and the beautiful naturally go hand in hand, as the ancient Greeks believed. Whatever the truth of the matter, Kirwan is an excellent place to spend an afternoon meditating on the subject.

The fine family charterhouse (right, top), with its porch and charming bed of climbing roses (right, center), contains salons decorated with appealing touches which evoke the cultural heritage of the Médoc region (facing page).

CHÂTEAU
D'ISSAN

Margaux

That this third-ranked *grand cru classé* is part of history is hard to deny. Issan wines were served at Eleanor of Aquitaine's wedding to Henry Plantagenet; Austrian Emperor Franz Josef ordered it for his table at the Hofburg. And, lastly, this great wine's motto, *Regum mensis arisque deorum* ("For the tables of kings and the altars of the gods"), presumptuous as it may seem, is nonetheless apt. No one doubts the historic credentials of Issan.

It is also true that the estate's fine château forms part of France's artistic heritage. Visitors are immediately impressed by the imposing wall that surrounds the property and endows the vineyard with a kind of sacred atmosphere rarely found in the Médoc region outside Latour. The château itself possesses all the charms associated with the finest seventeenth-century architecture, and appears on the supplementary listing of French historic monuments. Everything on the estate, including the old wine cellars with their ship's-hull ceiling beams, contributes to a magnificent setting used for the concerts presented as part of the "Musique au Cœur du Médoc" festival.

These are permanent features of the estate. However, for the new generation of the Cruse family—and especially for youthful Emmanuel, who has been orchestrating the estate's modernization since 1998—"history" and "heritage" can have their disadvantages. They need to be kept in their place, in any case. This is because, for too long, the site's inherent prestige partly obscured the acquired deficiencies of a wine whose high reputation no longer reflected reality.

It should be pointed out that Emmanuel Cruse, despite his name, had never before held a position of responsibility in the Bordeaux wine trade. But he decided to take the plunge, to adopt as his own his passion for making great wines, and to devote himself body and soul to what can only be called the resurrection of the family estate. This is why one is not surprised to find that he would rather discuss the technicalities of viticulture than the finer points of historic architecture. Fair enough—he deserves credit for harboring a passion focused entirely on a heavenly product.

It's also true that, at Issan, the weight of the past can sometimes be a stumbling-block on the road to efficient

This château, reflected in its broad moats,
is an outstanding gem of regional architecture.

modernization. For example: when it became time to renovate the winery, new production equipment had to be squeezed into the existing buildings, fitted inside structures that could not be changed in any way. This feat was something like assembling a Rubik's cube—a lot easier said than done.

Emmanuel Cruse, with admirable courage and determination, has embarked on systematic change. With the able assistance of Jacques Boissenot, they have gradually improved everything that could be improved. Today they are reaping their reward: the ability to produce a wine that satisfies the most demanding palates. They faced a challenge, and they met it. The greatest wine critics in the world, including Broadbent and Parker, have revised their former opinions, and are again ranking Issan among the best of Margaux wines. In the words of one such connoisseur, as reported in the June 1999 issue of *Le Monde des*

Grands Bordeaux, "Young Emmanuel Cruse has been working on the quality of Issan wine for several years now, and he is to be congratulated. His wines exhibit considerable charm, with aromas that are both mature and unaggressive."

If you, too, would like to compliment the Issan team, here is a word to the wise: compliment the wine, not the buildings. You'll have plenty of time, later, to wander through the grounds at your leisure, appreciating the unique charms of one of the most delightful estates in the region.

The old postern-gate (left) and dovecote (above, right) tend to make us forget the recent improvements to the modern and efficient winery (above, left).

145

CHÂTEAU
LAGRANGE

Saint-Julien

With a total area of around 390 acres (157 hectares), including over 270 acres (110 hectares) planted in vineyards, Lagrange is undisputedly the giant of the *grand cru classé* estates. The property was even larger back in 1855, when it covered over 740 acres (300 hectares)—a record for this region, where most estates have generally been smaller. Lagrange actually once contained an entire privately owned village, with its own bakery, school, and church.

This is an ancient property. The noble house of Lagrange Monteil, a part of which was attached to the Commanderie du Temple de Bordeaux, already produced a highly reputed wine back in the Middle Ages. An ancient property, and an illustrious one. It was directed by highly placed dignitaries, notably Comte Cabarrus, Joseph Bonaparte's finance minister in Spain, and Comte Duchâtel, who served a term as Louis-Philippe's minister of the interior.

In 1925 the estate was purchased by a Basque family from San Sebastian, the Cendoyas. It is said that the estate's wines had by then deteriorated so badly, the only reason anyone would have wanted to acquire Lagrange was to cut down its pine forests and market the wood to paper mills. A sad era indeed. Lagrange continued to decline, suffering financial losses and depreciation. The estate was a mere shadow of its former self when the Japanese group Suntory, a world leader in the alcoholic beverage industry, assumed control in 1983.

Worst of all, the best parcels of land, which had lain fallow for several years, had not been replanted. There was thus no way the estate could demonstrate its potential. Everything had to be restored, reorganized, recreated. There was nevertheless a glimmer of hope for the future, based on the prime asset constituted by the estate's vast area. Also, the new investors had a clear and demanding vision of how to go about fulfilling this inherent potential.

With praiseworthy constancy, these Japanese owners provided the large infusions of capital required for refloating the foundering ship, the largest in the Médoc armada, to be sure, but also the most dilapidated. They were clear-sighted enough to understand the need for a long-term strategy, and did not seek quick profits or immediate returns

The cleaned and enlarged pond adds the perfect touch
of romanticism to the château.

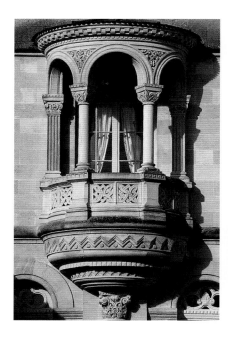   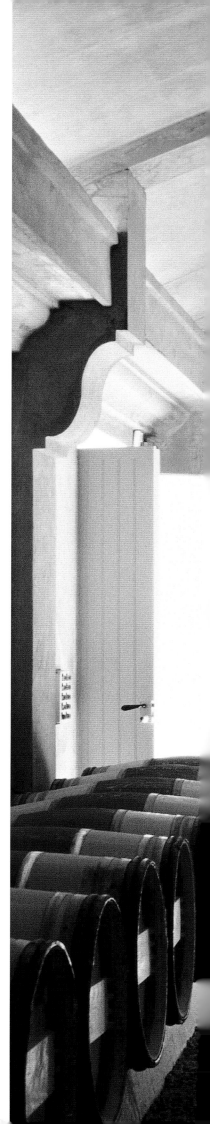

on their investment. The Lagrange treasury continued to register a deficit for over a decade, until 1996.

The good news for Suntory—as its representatives are the first to admit today—was being able to count on the skills of a director like Marcel Ducasse. With Dr. Peynaud as his mentor, this virtuoso of the vineyard was able not only to breathe new life into the moribund vines, but also to extract from their fruit a rare wine exhibiting the true soul of a *grand cru*. Some idea of Ducasse's originality can be formed simply from noting the importance given under his tutelage to that most capricious of rootstocks, Petit Verdot. Other wines may contain a barely perceptible trace of this variety, but at Lagrange it constitutes fully one-fifth of the blends.

Over the years, Suntory's Japanese leaders have maintained their trust in Ducasse, a man who has never stooped to doing things the easy way just to impress them. Like his supporters' antecedents in the Land of the Rising Sun, he

has kept one foot placed firmly in the traditional past, the other pointing ahead to a progressive future. His assistant, Bruno Eynard, is eloquent on the subject: "On this estate," he tells us, "there are places where we work exactly as people did a hundred years ago or more; then there are others where we do just the opposite, where everything has changed very recently. And when I say 'very recently,'" he adds, "I mean less than fifteen months ago."

Loggia, watchtower . . . Nineteenth-century ornamentation lends a picturesque note to the house (above). But the most imposing installations lie elsewhere: in the gigantic cellars (right), designed to accommodate one of the largest productions of wine in the region.

CHÂTEAU
LANGOA BARTON

Saint-Julien

Anthony Barton has an air of casual elegance belonging to an experienced host. He receives you warmly with no apparent effort, but with the gift—so appreciated in these days of ill manners—of making you feel at home somewhere you hardly knew at all a couple of hours before. The decor, both comfortable and elegent, has a distinct classic Irish feel. It accompanies with harmony the delicious Médoc meal served on silver plates by stylish staff.

In the aristocratic features of the proprietor, you can at once perceive the family resemblance to the portraits of ancestors dating back some three hundred years. You cannot help commenting. "Really?" says your host with feigned surprise: "You noticed?" Less courteous, he might have quite simply reminded you of his distinguished ancestry, but he refrains from doing so.

Anthony Barton was born in 1930 in County Kildare at Staffran House, the house acquired a century before by his ancestor, Hugh Barton. This astute businessman was the grandson of Thomas Barton, "French Tom" as he was known, who founded in 1722 the Bordeaux house that bore his name. Hugh Barton subsequently purchased Château Langoa in 1821. These two activities, wine merchant and producer, have been perpetuated by the Bartons up to the present day, an unusual situation worth mentioning.

Anthony Barton is a younger son, and, as such, was not predestined to be heir to the vineyards. However, his uncle did not marry until late in life and had no children. He chose Anthony to be his heir and donated both Langoa and Léoville Barton to him in 1983, "just three years before he died," as Anthony mentioned. Uncle Ronald was a great personality, both reserved and gregarious. He came to Bordeaux in 1924 following a classical education at Eton, and Oxford. During World War II he served as a British liaison officer with the Free French forces far from the family firm of Barton & Guestier and his two vineyards in Saint-Julien. But he returned with new energy and enthusiasm in 1945, producing such great vintages as 1948 and 1949.

When his nephew Anthony expressed gratitude for

The Château, where the Barton family still entertain so charmingly, has changed little since the time when this Sèvres dish was painted.

such a splendid legacy, he replied, "It is not me you should thank but Hugh. I have always considered myself to be guardian of the vineyards with a duty to pass them on to my heir in the best possible condition." A principle that Anthony can adopt for his own account. Following the accidental death of his son, Thomas, it is his daughter, Lilian Barton-Sartorius who is following in the family footsteps. She already manages the wine firm created by her father in 1967.

In the Barton home everything seems to happen naturally. One breathes the purest air, that of ease and simplicity.

Lunch comes to a quiet close to the melodious notes of a great vintage and you realize that the admirable "Chartreuse" Château, whose façade decorates the label of Léoville, classified a Second Growth, actually belongs to Langoa, a Third Growth.

So where are you? At Château Léoville Barton? At Château Langoa Barton? You are not going to create problems over such a small detail. With very British—or more precisely Irish—tact you will consider, with no risk of error, that this divine house should be called quite simply "Château Barton."

The imposing buildings lining the "Route du Vin" (above) contain the most prestigious oak vats in Saint-Julien (right).

CHÂTEAU
GISCOURS

Margaux

The tiny pebbles embedded in the floor of the old cellar glint in the light cast by a sunbeam slanting through the slit between the heavy dark-red door and the rough brick walls. On the walls hang timeless utensils, silent witnesses to an activity that is surely immemorial. Although Bordeaux is less than twelve miles (twenty kilometers) away, the estate seems completely isolated. We might believe ourselves lost in the past. Giscours sparkles serenely in the sunshine outside.

The estate was built and then rebuilt one stone at a time by a long series of owners. It is said that in 1330 a fortified donjon marked the presence here of powerful feudal lords, but the first record of vineyards being planted dates from the middle of the sixteenth century. Later, while traveling with his mother in 1654, during the Fronde insurrection, Louis XIV is said to have tasted the great Giscours wine and expressed his appreciation. The French Revolution could easily have swept all this away, but it actually extended the Saint-Simon family trusteeship of an estate that had already been through turbulent times. In 1795 the property—like so many others—was remanded to the nation.

Giscours was given a fresh start under the July Monarchy, and considerable progress had been made by the time of the 1855 rankings. However, it was not until the Second Empire that celebrated Parisian banker Comte Pescatore had the château completely rebuilt, ostensibly in order to provide a fitting stopover for the Empress Eugénie during her journey to Biarritz. The château itself was not the only feature of the estate benefiting from this renovation. New and functionally planned outbuildings contained vast and hygienic spaces dedicated to specific purposes—as the self-explanatory inscriptions reading "cellars" and "stables" carved over the stone lintels on either side of the courtyard still attest today.

But it was not until much nearer our own time that ambitious new projects were initiated at Giscours. It is common knowledge that when the Taris acquired the estate in 1952, the vineyard was in steep decline, the outbuildings

*Set somewhat apart from the château, the villa offers charms that proved irresistible
to esthetes like Monsieur and Madame Albada Jilgersma.*

crumbling, and the château itself in an advanced state of decrepitude. Nicolas Tari and, later, his son Pierre deserve full credit for taking things in hand, pulling the estate back from the brink of disaster, and rebuilding. It is Nicolas Tari who created the famous artificial lake covering some twenty-five acres (ten hectares) that is now completely integrated into the site. The lake is not only ornamental but has the additional advantage of promoting a favorable microclimate by humidifying the air around it.

In 1994, serious financial difficulties forced the owners to sell the estate to new investors. For Giscours, this signaled a new leap forward. The Dutch businessman Eric Albada Jelgersma became deeply interested in the property and did all he could to restore the vineyard, the château, and the outbuildings. In less than a decade, a significant amount of capital was injected into an enterprise with solid foundations that had previously lacked the means for

making a fresh start. Today, visitors to Giscours have every reason to appreciate the taste of the new owners, as reflected in the resort-style villa a short distance away and the hospitable guest rooms skillfully constructed inside the restored outbuildings. These Dutch francophiles—who also own Le Tertre—have made the revival, or resurrection, of Giscours a family affair. Even better: it's the focus of their existence.

From the château's carved ridge tiles (left),
to the elaborate stone trophies (above, center),
the estate's buildings illustrate a Second-Empire
conception of what a great wine-growing estate
should look like.

CHÂTEAU
MALESCOT SAINT-EXUPÉRY

Margaux

"*Semper ad altum.*" "Ever higher." True to its motto—and to its famous name—this *troisième grand cru* has eschewed facility and chosen the rocky path of discipline and high aspirations. In fact, Antoine de Saint-Exupéry, the author of *The Little Prince*, whose distant ancestor Jean-Baptiste acquired the estate in 1827, stated in precisely these terms his own view of achievement through struggle: "Obstacles are liberating; they provide the only freedom worth having"—the magnificent freedom of difficulties met and overcome.

In the opinion of Jean-Luc Zuger, third member of the dynasty that has reigned for the past half-century over Malescot, the brilliant success of the great Margaux wines is a phenomenon too recent to be taken for granted. Zuger, a still youthful man with twinkling eyes and a rough fisherman's beard, has not forgotten the slump of the 1960s, when the profit from the sale of wine produced on one acre (half a hectare) of good vineyard was just about enough to pay for a modest TV set or washing machine. He learned the lesson taught by hard times, and knows how to set his priorities. "I invest everything in the winery, the equipment, and the vineyard itself," he says. He's keenly and continually aware that a wine's greatness depends on small details. He and his attentive team are meticulously respectful of ancient principles and methods. Fermentation is slow and lengthy; the wine is circulated in the vats before, during, and after fermentation.

Malescot is one of the all-too-rare estates on which "house" rules are respected. This is a matter of legitimate pride: "The tiered fermenting room, which has been copied everywhere, was invented here," Zuger notes in passing.

Until very recently a notable aspect of this wine was that—unusually and even uniquely for a vintage of this quality—it was not placed on the Bordeaux market. Thirty years of independently conducted sales have at least confirmed the estate's master in his healthy attitude of detachment from the system, his frank autonomy. More generally, there is also a tendency at Malescot Saint-Exupéry to be

A real authenticity is what makes this wine-producing estate so charming.

... dans mes estudes a ... und ...

de maistres Jaques greuier secrettaire ...

... al a de preue deuant quar tenir ...

bord ... a Cre 2 ...

... mal de ... aug ...

Fontanes ... Royal

1er Août 1697.

... de l'acquisition

... sans prejudic...

... en mesme ...

GEN·DE·BORDEAVX

Sachent tous presens ...

II

wary of passing fashion—including the frenetic emulation that impels some vintners to concoct wines specifically calculated to win tasting competitions. "A wine should be made for people to drink, not for experts to taste," is the philosophy here.

According to Jean-Luc Zuger, the current wine market suffers from two conflicting and inflated trends. The first is speculation, which encourages uninformed consumers to invest in cases of wine the way others invest in expensive works of art; the second is the chronic impatience of people unwilling to wait until wines have fully matured, eager to drink them long before their full aroma and bouquet have had a chance to develop. To counter this dual trend would require training, experience, and the gradual acquisition of discriminating taste on the part of consumers. Unfortunately, the times are not particularly favorable to the development of connoisseurship on this level.

Here at Malescot Saint-Exupéry, at least, no one dreams of succumbing to facility and the fad for more immediately accessible wines. This estate is exemplary for its slowly matured wine; the men who make it are determined to endow it with the kind of staying power that requires patient cellar aging. The metallic flavor Malescot Saint-Exupéry acquires after long aging and—according to the experts—shares only with Mouton, may come as a surprise to neophytes, but is thoroughly relished by that crucially important minority able to enjoy it with the true appreciation of connoisseurs.

This great estate has preserved from its illustrious past not only a number of attractive buildings and some antique bottles (right), but also—alas, a rarity— archives that are virtually complete (facing page).

CHÂTEAU
BOYD-CANTENAC

Margaux

The long and illustrious history of Boyd-Cantenac has been marked by a number of great names, like illuminated letters illustrating the pages of a medieval manuscript. The estate was founded in the village of Cantenac by Jacques Boyd, a nobleman of Irish origin, in the mid-eighteenth century. It was then acquired by a wealthy English gentleman and amateur watercolorist, John Lewis-Brown. He brought a touch of fantasy and imagination that is occasionally lacking in some estates that play everything by the book. It then passed into the Ginestet family, who enhanced the estate's already fine reputation by adding the depth and soul without which a Third Growth *grand cru* would be but a shadow of itself.

Château Boyd-Cantenac has been in the family of the current owner, Lucien Guillemet, for three generations—since 1932, to be precise. The family had already acquired the neighboring lands of Pouget a good twenty-five years previously. It is not too much to say that the new owners bought Boyd-Cantenac as an easy way of expanding their property rather than for its vines. In those days, the land had been clumsily divided between various family members and had neither a château nor its own wine cellar. To this day, its fine wines are aged in the Pouget cellars, which are themselves delightfully rough-hewn, full of a simple country charm that is perhaps more typical of Burgundy than the Médoc.

The remarkable qualities of the soil and a careful choice of grape varieties make for a subtle Third Growth *grand cru* whose bouquet, in particular, is strikingly unusual. Lucien Guillemet takes great care to preserve the individual character of the Boyd and Pouget vintages. The Boyd vintage contains approximately 8 percent of Cabernet Franc, giving it a refined, smooth character. The Pouget vintage has more body and the tannins are more to the fore. Boyd wines have a velvety finesse and smoothness that is very much in line with current tastes in wine, while remaining faithful to the historical character of the estate.

Lucien Guillemet is not the sort of man to believe that sophisticated vinification techniques can perform miracles. He has a very free, almost bohemian, outlook on life, which means he is happy to trust to nature to produce a great wine. This is surely what gives Boyd-Cantenac and Pouget wines such charm and authenticity. Their regular clients, all true connoisseurs, are particularly fond of the charming simplicity of their wines, which Lucien Guillemet intends to maintain as the signature of his estate, whatever the future might hold in store.

The inscriptions cut into the stone medallions on the pediment of this charming house
are historically inexact—which makes them even more appealing.

It is to small—some might say insignificant—details that great estates owe
an essential part of their magic. For example, meticulously etched corks (facing page)
and these marvelous glass plugs used on the casks that hold the new harvest (above).

CHÂTEAU
CANTENAC BROWN

Margaux

In hushed silence, José Sanfins concentrates all of his attention on the battalion of wine-tasting glasses ranged on a long white table before him. Now and then he pours a few drops of ruby liquid into a graduated test tube, adds another from a different lot, and then a third, gently swirling the resulting mixture. He tastes, deliberates, makes a slight adjustment, adds a tiny bit of something else, tastes again, sniffs, "chews," and then finally sets his glass down with the unmistakable gesture of a man who has made up his mind. "This time," he declares, "I think we have our blend." Here is a very special moment in a year of varied and complementary tasks—the most crucial moment of all. For, unlike chefs, the creators of great vintage wines have only one opportunity per year to exhibit their talents. If they fail, they do not get a second chance.

Portuguese native José Sanfins has been technical director of the estate since 1989. A man who travels widely and is incurably inquisitive about everything that goes on in the world, Sanfins is living proof of the openness and modernity characteristic of Cantenac Brown. He belongs to the new generation of vintners—people like Emmanuel Cruse, John Kolasa, Gonzague Lurton, and Paul Pontallier—that has recreated the Margaux *appellation*. These young, capable men are not interested in sterile competition and underhanded backbiting. A healthy and even amicable spirit of emulation has replaced the old feuds and, combined with current market imperatives, is forging a truly positive attitude in this venerable and noble wineproducing region.

As it happens, in 1989 the Compagnie du Midi, which had owned Cantenac Brown for two years past, merged with AXA. As a result, this somewhat lackluster *troisième cru* joined the famous insurance group's other estates, taking up a position behind Pichon-Longueville in the AXA Millésimes subsidiary. This was good news for connoisseurs of great wine. In just a few years, Cantenac Brown shed the relative harshness for which it had been criticized in recent years, recovering a mellowness and balance fully worthy of its immemorial reputation.

The numerous châteaux in the Médoc region which deserve the name "grande maison"
owe this to their princely succession of formal salons—here marred by inappropriate furnishings.

Today, under the direction of managing director Christian Seely, a concern for the environment is reflected at Cantenac Brown by intensive work on the vineyard—a global effort rewarded in 2002 with the coveted quality certification. Pruning, disbudding, and thinning of the vines are accompanied by meticulous monitoring of the organic fertilizers used and a return to traditional agricultural methods. Entire parcels of land have been replanted. "We try to adapt the rootstock to the soil," explains José Sanfins. "It's a long-term project. It will be thirty years before the vineyards I'm planting today mature."

The estate is thus returning to the customs and methods of its great era. Could this resurrection someday be extended to the sumptuous realm of fêtes and receptions? We should not forget, in any case, that in former times—and particularly under the Second Empire—the estate's then owner, Armand Lalande, followed the lead of the great hedonist John Lewis-Brown in offering opulent evening entertainments to society's elite. On those occasions, the vast manor in the British public school mock-Tudor style was a beacon of glorious light. The muffled sound of laughter and animated conversation echoed in the vineyards and off into the dark Médoc night.

*Despite its British public-school-style façade (top)—
reproduced on the great wine's labels—and salons frozen
in the late nineteenth century (bottom), this property's extensive
buildings also house modern fermenting vats (center) and
an ultra-contemporary swimming pool (facing page)
installed for the pleasure of the estate's special guests.*

CHÂTEAU
PALMER

Margaux

Gold and midnight blue: Palmer's two emblematic colors reflect the image of a great vintage wine that is both timelessly elegant and totally contemporary. On the one hand, the noblest of traditions anchored in a soil that experts rank among the best of any; on the other, a spirit of discovery and even adventure, supported by innovative methods and symbolized in visible form by the somewhat fanciful architecture of the château itself—an exuberant fairy-tale castle ornamented with elaborate gingerbread on its steep roof. The theme is continued in the vineyard itself, which is planted with a combination of Merlot and Cabernet Sauvignon that, while faithfully reflecting some of this vintage's traditions, nevertheless expresses an innovative daring that few of the great names in the Margaux region could claim.

Palmer owes its legendary name and remarkable soil to a major-general in the British army who acquired the Gascq estate in 1814 and proceeded to raise it to the heights of excellence. Fortunately for him, a solid basis for his endeavor was already in place: during the previous century, the quality of the estate's great wine won it a place on tables at the court of Louis XV. However, it was not until the arrival of famed Second Empire bankers Emile and Isaac Pereire in 1853 that Palmer truly came into its own. In 1855, bringing to the management of their estate all the energy deployed throughout their vast railway and commercial empire, the two brothers created an extensive market for this third-ranked *grand cru classé*—but they didn't tamper with well-established methods. Tradition combined with modernity is a dialectic clearly etched from the start in the Palmer genes.

The torch was subsequently passed to a consortium uniting the inevitable Bordeaux families with investors from the Netherlands and Great Britain, and this group maintained the subtle balance that gives this outstanding wine the refined character expressing the greatness of its soil.

To meet this challenge, Palmer has embarked on major innovations, such as stainless-steel casks with heat-regulated conic bodies. Improved analysis of each parcel of land reflects an extensive geological study conducted throughout the vineyard for the purpose of exploring deeper levels of

A cellar such as this sums up
the entire historic past of a great wine.

the sub-soil for the purpose of analyzing with scientific accuracy some empirically observed phenomena whose causes had hitherto been little understood. There are some who might rail against such arrogant attempts to extend the boundaries of knowledge and deal more effectively with the vagaries of nature; however, those who understand the Palmer spirit and its perennial daring will not be unduly surprised.

Today, although weather patterns and the diseases that threaten vines may still not be under complete control, they are better understood than in the past. In view of this, it would thus be unthinkable for an estate with a pioneering tradition to lag behind others. Scientific analysis of a soil universally but vaguely termed "excellent" was imperative. It will now be apparent why this "excellent" soil produces such great wines. However, scientific precision will never interfere with the amazement and delight connoisseurs will still feel in response to a great Margaux like Palmer.

Located within the city of Margaux, the château (top) is surrounded by the winery buildings. Despite the execution of much-needed renovations, the buildings have preserved all the charm of their storied past.

CHÂTEAU
LA LAGUNE

Haut-Médoc

There are some secretive, slightly obscure estates that surrender to the gaze and appreciation of outsiders only after delicate and sometimes tortuous negotiation. But La Lagune is not one of them, not in any way at all. Here there is no obfuscation as visitors are led to the easily accessible, clearly visible vineyard—the very first on the "Route des Châteaux du Médoc" leading out of Bordeaux. The house itself seems simple and unpretentious, a fine eighteenth-century charterhouse in the perfectly unadorned neoclassic style practiced by the architect of Bordeaux's Grand Théâtre, Victor Louis.

The fact that the estate's current owners come from the world of Champagne is seen here as a somewhat exotic anomaly. This came about because La Lagune was once owned by René Chayoux, president of Ayala Champagnes. Jean-Michel Ducellier—the man who had so ably assisted Réné Chayoux for twenty years past—assumed the leadership of La Lagune. Later his own son, Alain Ducellier, decided to continue the task of restoring the estate to its proper rank, a position it should never have lost.

The situation of La Lagune was already seen by many as dire when René Chayoux decided to purchase it. "You had to be crazy to do it," declared eminent wine connoisseur Alexis Lichine, who nevertheless expressed frank admiration for that kind of madness. It must be said that in the past the estate had a tendency to shrink like the disappearing cloak in the fairy tale. As the cultivated area diminished, the challenge of possible acquisition became more difficult to meet. But it would have taken a lot more than that to discourage the people from Champagne. Under their stewardship, the estate began its gradual recovery.

In 2000 a new chapter opened in the La Lagune story. The arrival at the helm of Thierry Budin, assisted by oenologist Caroline Frey, disciple of Professor Denis Dubourdieu, infused fresh energy into restructuring the vineyard and renovating the winery. La Lagune was clearly turning over a new leaf, but the depressing legacy of the past was not by any means obliterated. Minor improvements made over the previous decades were scrupulously maintained and extended. But surely this is the prerequisite for truly lasting success.

A fine horseshoe staircase—a miniature version of the "Fontainebleau" style— lends great nobility to this small charterhouse.

The most spectacular feature of the renovated La Lagune is its brand-new fermenting room. Imagine an immense semicircular room where two long tubes move like the hands of a clock in a sweeping horizontal motion, supplying wine in an arc to a tier of gleaming stainless-steel vats. This vintner's dream come true was first conceived in the fertile mind of architect Patrick Baggio, highly reputed in the region. Although high-tech in appearance and in fact, this equipment actually designed to exploit the force of gravity represents the continuation of what had already become a local tradition. The first ultra-modern fermenting room in the region was inaugurated as far back as 1961. It was revolutionary for its time and not immediately accepted by all. But it established a new tradition for the production of great wine: a slightly different one, perhaps; but just as stylish, certainly.

Through a play of contrasts, the new, ultra-modern, semi-circular winery underscores the charms of the old monogrammed door at the end of the château's shady avenue, and courtyards which need only the ghost of an antique horse-drawn carriage to complete the picture (facing page).

CHÂTEAU
DESMIRAIL

Margaux

The Desmirail story is an exciting one. Featuring high drama, breathtaking suspense, and sudden changes of fortune, it really should be followed from beginning to end, but the last chapter is the most gripping. The important thing to bear in mind is that this proud Margaux wine with a well-earned reputation for elegance once held an uncontested place among the third-ranked *grands crus* of the 1855 classification. And then, over time, through transfers and legacies, it eventually faded almost to nothing. Failing the test of time, only its name survived—but even the name carried less and less weight as the years went by. The vineyard was taken over by the vast Palmer estate; the château and its outbuildings were unexpectedly acquired by the Marquis d'Alesme. *Sic transit gloria mundi . . .*

We might note in passing that the estate owes its prestigious name, Desmirail, to a seventeenth-century lawyer whose huge fortune won him the hand in marriage of a certain demoiselle Rauzan. Today another lawyer, Denis Lurton, has given up the bar in order to devote himself to

the estate, to guide the fortunes of a property that has literally been raised from the dead. And that's our final chapter to date: Resurrection. This was not accomplished in a day, of course. It took place in gradual stages orchestrated by Denis's father, the indefatigable Lucien Lurton. Starting in 1960, he deployed strict discipline and endless patience in the systematic reconstruction of the forty-five-acre (eighteen-hectare) vineyard on an estate eminently worthy of the high ranking it had received in better times. Lurton even acquired a number of fine buildings in the commune of Cantenac and proceeded to renovate them. For example: the main gate is flanked by monumental columns made of Languedoc marble (a favorite of Louis XIV and Hardouin-Mansart); the winery has recovered its native beauty; and, for its part, the château, built of lovely pale-colored stone, has been given a carved pediment which makes it the most elegant of neoclassic charterhouses. It appears today on the labels gracing this great wine's bottles. Having been released from the limbo to which it had been consigned, Desmirail

*The majestic door of the new château reflects
a very ancient tradition.*

was to become a source of pride to its former—and illustrious—proprietors. The latter included, among others, Berlin banker Robert von Mendelssohn, nephew of the composer and (more importantly) grandson of the famed Biarnez known in this region as the "bard of the vines." It is regrettable that Biarnez, a great connoisseur of Médoc wines during their Golden Age, is not with us now to dash off a few lines in honor of Desmirail in its new guise. It is a curious enterprise—and a daring one—to restore a château, a winery, and a vineyard to the former glory of what in recent years had become just an empty name. A prestigious and once proud name, to be sure, but one that had been emptied of significance over the years.

In our view, Denis Lurton would be wrong to minimize the breadth of his achievement. Far from tarnishing the brilliance of his estate, his restoration has endowed it with an almost magical aura. This is especially true in that, by improving Desmirail wine to a level of impeccable classicism now recognized by demanding connoisseurs as readily as they recognize the harmonious proportions of the charterhouse, he has succeeded in burnishing the estate's escutcheon anew. Better yet, and against heavy odds, he has met the huge challenge of forging new links with the traditional virtues of a wine habitually prized for its balance rather than its strength.

*Across from the old cask cellars (left) stands
the extensively remodeled charterhouse featuring a fine,
recently added ornamental façade (above).*

CHÂTEAU
CALON SÉGUR

Saint-Estèphe

This morning there's a small fire crackling merrily in the fireplace of the salon-vestibule. Comfortable yet elegant and tasteful furnishings contribute to the intimate feeling of the entire house. Outdoors the skies are gray, but inside the atmosphere is sunny. We are with the cheerful and energetic Madame Capbern-Gasqueton, who is explaining how profoundly she's attached to the estate. It's true, indeed, that this northernmost château of the Médoc region is undeniably the most bewitching of all. The gently rolling vineyard enclosed by timeless walls; the unadorned, ideally proportioned, and hospitable château; the unobtrusive, functional winery—everything at Calon Ségur combines to reinforce the harmony of the site and the beauty of the estate. Magnificent!

It comes as no surprise that the Marquis de Ségur, "Prince of the Vines," whose ghost has accompanied our visit from the beginning, had a soft spot in his heart for this unique place. "I produce wine at Lafite and Latour," he often said, "but my heart is at Calon." His face, if not his heart, is still here: engraved on a stone medallion gracing the façade of the old winery, and as a stylized figure on the label of his great wine—a joy to romantic Japanese consumers and Saint Valentine's Day lovers. An unheard-of, and unique, concession to the marketing imperatives of an era whose worst abuses have not yet come this far.

With the affable energy of a self-confident person, the owner, Madame Capbern-Gasqueton next guides us on a tour of the extensive gardens and a fine orangery with aromatic shrubs, toward the ultramodern winery—an integral but well-hidden component of her domain.

Here, without undue fuss, some 200,000 bottles of the greatest Saint-Estèphe are produced annually. The body and bouquet of this wine have consistently beguiled the palates of connoisseurs, to the point where some vintages occupy that supreme rank where oenological myths are made.

Let us venture farther and try to unveil the secrets of an estate where production appears to occur almost effortlessly. First, it is worth mentioning that the 135 acres (55 hectares) of the enclosed vineyard are the same ones

Seen from the distant vantage-point of the vineyard,
the pure lines of the mansion evoke those of romanesque basilicas.

planted when the ranking was first awarded—an additional proof of continuity. Naturally, the entire area is not in production at any one time: some sections are in various stages of development. But none are planted with anything but grapevines. Each section is monitored carefully so that harvesting can take place at the optimum moment, which depends on the relative maturity of the Cabernet Sauvignon grapes that form the lion's share of the estate's rootstock. Uprooting here is minimal in order to preserve what is essential—the harmonious expression of an admirable soil.

"Our job is not to produce prize-winning wines, but to offer loyal consumers of our great wine something that will be a pleasure to drink. Abstract analysis should never go beyond a certain point." The more closely one listens to the soul of this estate, the more a concept of coherence emerges. Calon Ségur is an integrated whole, a harmonious and living ensemble in which the perfection of the landscape, the beauty of the buildings, the discreet positioning of the win-

ery installations, and the charm of generous-hearted bottles each add their voice to a polyphonic chorus.

It would be treason to attempt to separate these various components and analyze their specific alchemy. The essential resides in a somewhat hazy, somewhat distant overall view. A view that respects the estate's mystery and keeps it alive and vibrant over the long term.

Visitors viewing this château (right and above, left) easily understand how it stole the heart of the "Prince of Vines". The cask cellars are partially buried, mainly in order to preserve the esthetic harmony of the site (above, right).

CHÂTEAU
FERRIÈRE

Margaux

The oldest, the largest, the finest, the northernmost, the southernmost: superlatives are common currency in the highly competitive Médoc region, where every estate claims one as its own. Ferrière's superlative is a disarmingly modest one, however. This is the smallest of the estates producing a *grand cru* listed in the 1855 rankings. The smallest of all, with a vineyard covering fewer than twenty acres (eight hectares). The smallest of all, with a château no bigger than a fair-sized villa. In a word: the smallest.

Claire Villars-Lurton adopted a brilliant strategy to deal with this. She turned smallness into an asset. Knowing that some weaknesses, if acknowledged and properly exploited, can be transformed into strengths, as the estate's new owner she underscored the advantages of her acquisition's minute size. Her strategy is similar to that of great chefs who display their creations in cramped dining rooms. "A precious little gem on a velvet cushion," is how the woman who has presided over the château's fortunes since 1992 describes it.

Ferrière is not only small, it has also suffered a period of eclipse. To be sure, it owes its name to one of the great landowning families under the ancien régime, but the Ferrières did not survive World War I unscathed. After them came the deluge . . . or, rather, the desert. The prestigious name and even the label remained, but the practice of using outside wineries for vinification—first Prieuré-Lichine, then Lascombe—reduced this great *premier cru* to second-class status. Under the circumstances, the eventual rise of the phoenix from its ashes was bound to attract notice. The realization of a once widely recognized potential and the return to top status of a wine that had languished for decades is an exciting development. Ferrière, a precious little gem indeed, but one cast into outer darkness, has finally emerged into the light and now sparkles with a thousand fiery gleams, paradoxically—but with a kind of poetic justice—benefiting from its all too lengthy somnolence. Good news! Sleeping Beauty has been roused. But this time the

Palm trees add an unmistakably Italian touch
to this lovely façade.

sleeper is a prince, awakened by the magic kiss of a princess: Claire Villars-Lurton.

With rare speed and skill, the new team has brilliantly succeeded in reforging Ferrière's link with the past and recovering a reputation which should never have been lost: that of a very great dark, almost black, wine with an admirable and extremely subtle floral-spice bouquet.

Ferrière's saviors were forced to start again from scratch—sometimes a blessing in disguise—and they began by devoting most of their efforts to restoring health to the foundation on which all else is built: the soil and the root-stock, or, in local parlance, the "raw material." Proceeding homeopathically rather than allopathically, as it were, the team has gradually regained total control over this small vineyard, which is split up—atomized would be a better word—among several different communes in the Margaux region.

Without this basic foundation-work, the miracle of Ferrière would no doubt never have taken place. But that work was only the beginning. Achieving the miracle has also required daring, discipline, patience, and perhaps a little alchemy—or magic.

Decorated in the style of the 1940s, the dining room (facing page) projects a frivolity also found in the paneled turret (top, right) and on the labels (bottom, right).

CHÂTEAU
MARQUIS D'ALESME BECKER

Margaux

When one visits all the *grand cru classé* estates in the Médoc, as I have been privileged to do, one's reactions are more often admiration and enthusiasm than surprise or amazement. But Marquis d'Alesme is truly amazing, a virtue for which its current owner, Jean-Claude Zuger, deserves all the credit.

The first pleasant surprise is the house itself. This elegant mid-nineteenth-century edifice designed in an appealing Louis XIII style, although located right in the middle of the village of Margaux, carefully conceals its brick-and-stone façade from indiscreet eyes. The elongated structure actually forms a right angle with the village's main street, and this makes it hard to see from the entrance gate.

The second, no less pleasant, surprise: the cellars and winery. In the late twentieth century, extensive modernization work was undertaken on installations crying out for renovation. A stainless-steel fermenting vat equipped with a cutting-edge heat-regulation system, an insulated and air-conditioned storage cellar, and ideally arranged tasting and meeting rooms lie concealed under the traditional exteriors of the old buildings.

Another pleasant surprise, and not by any means the least: a vineyard significantly enlarged by the addition of seventeen acres (seven hectares) formerly rented out to Malescot Saint-Exupéry, thus increasing the area of arable land suitable for vineyards to a total of forty acres (sixteen hectares). Of this, twelve acres (five hectares) border the Château Margaux sector. Through yield limitation, manure reduction, selective leaf thinning, and noninvasive harvesting, a continual improvement in the quality of the grapes sent to the winery has been achieved.

There are thus many surprises in store for visitors who cross the threshold of Marquis d'Alesme Becker, and the biggest one of all is perhaps Jean-Claude Zuger himself. Zuger is a man whose warm personality and generous hospitality alone are the best spiritual nourishment the visitor

In olden times, people standing on the wooden turret could watch the great trading ships
as they sailed down the river to Les Chartrons.

could wish for. He's as happy as a child when showing off his wife's collection of fine crystal, the high-tech lighting in the new cellars, and the ingenious arrangement of the tasting room—including a counter made from a canoe.

To tell the truth, Zuger's glowing pride is the hard-won fruit of a fairly difficult past. The story begins with Jean-Claude Zuger's grandfather, Edmond Ritz, an engineer for the Alsatian potash mines. This prescient man sensed the coming disasters of World War II and moved his family to Margaux. His own son, Paul Zuger, subsequently acquired Malescot in the 1950s. On his death in 1979, Paul Zuger willed Malescot to his elder son Roger and Marquis d'Alesme to his younger son Jean-Claude.

This explains why Marquis d'Alesme Becker, a great wine classed *troisième grand cru* in the 1855 rankings, is produced in the buildings of what is now the Zugers' "parent company," Malescot. This is also the reason why everything

here needed to be renovated, if not totally re-created, starting with the construction of a modern winery and adequate cellars. In 2002, the Union des Grands Crus rewarded these years of laudable effort by integrating Jean-Claude Zuger's estate with its mighty and prestigious neighbor. Although this does not necessarily mean the estate is completely out of the woods, it does augur well for the future.

The labels of Marquis d'Alesme Becker have traditionally featured a horseshoe topped by the coronet of a marquis. May this horseshoe bring luck to the estate, and help it forward on the path to definitive consecration!

The Marquis d'Alesme was also "Equerry of Budos," which explains the omnipresence of horseshoes (above) on an estate whose façade (right) cannot be fully appreciated at a single glance.

Château Saint-Pierre

Château Talbot

Château Branaire-Ducru

Château Duhart-Milon

Château Pouget

Château La Tour Carnet

Château Lafon-Rochet

Château Beychevelle

Château Prieuré-Lichine

Château Marquis de Terme

CHÂTEAU
SAINT-PIERRE

Saint-Julien

The Bordeaux wine country has no shortage of estates called "Saint-Pierre." In order to distinguish this one from all the others, informed connoisseurs of Médoc tend to specify that it's the one originally known as "Saint-Pierre Sevaistre." Why Saint-Pierre? Because back in the time of Louis XV, the estate was purchased by a baron of the same name. When he died, the estate was divided between his two daughters and was not reunited until after World War I. Why Sevaistre? Because at the end of the nineteenth century, one of the two divisions was acquired by a man named Pierre Sevaistre.

It would be reasonable to assume that the renown of this *grand cru*, listed at the head of the fourth series in the 1855 rankings, might today be suffering slightly from the highly publicized proximity of Château Gloria *cru bourgeois*, flagship and jewel in the crown of the Martin estates. And, indeed, Gloria's success might well have eclipsed that of the vineyard next door had the two not been owned by the same man—a man concerned with avoiding exactly this sort of misplaced competition.

For it was this strategically placed neighbor, Henri Martin, who eventually assumed control of the by-then somnolent *grand cru* Saint-Pierre. In 1981 he joined forces with his daughter to buy an attractive estate owned by the Kapelhoff sisters. His purchase included a charterhouse built in the eighteenth century, tastefully enlarged during the nineteenth, and surrounded by a fine fifteen-acre (six-hectare) wooded park—an area spacious enough to accommodate a winery and cellar comfortably. "One thing leads to another," as the saying goes. The very next year Gloria's owner also acquired the vineyard itself: some forty-five acres (eighteen hectares) out of the approximately hundred acres (forty hectares) registered at the time of the 1855 rankings and located between the holdings of Gruaud Larose and those of Léoville and Beychevelle.

For a little over sixty years, the "old" Saint-Pierre had belonged to a family of wine merchants from Antwerp, the Van den Busches. Although this family installed a winery, the latter stands on lands today controlled by Ducru-Beaucaillou. It was thus imperative to endow the "new" Saint-Pierre with

The essence of the Médoc's spirit is to be found in this vestibule, which may appear slightly cold at first but is actually extremely hospitable.

production facilities worthy of its great wine, a project that inevitably involved the construction of entirely new buildings. Henri Martin assumed responsibility for the task, and architect Alain Triaud—who is related to the family and therefore seemed to be the perfect man for the job—set to work. Ground was broken, and a vast edifice—designed for producing and aging the three Martin wines—was soon rising from its foundations. Although the local authorities, particularly at the commune level, were at first reluctant to approve the project's innovative materials and design, the finished buildings represent a thoroughly successful example of a new winery skillfully integrated into an existing site.

This ultramodern facility is now used for the production of a nectar boasting an immemorial reputation, a great wine in the best Saint-Julien tradition, one of the most full-bodied in the region—a slightly tannic wine which, for that very reason, is expected to age magnificently. Its motto, *Nec Pluribus Impar*, was also the motto of Louis XIV. Potential competitors of Saint-Pierre might benefit from reflecting on the newly demonstrated merits of goals that were far from self-evident, and a success that has come late in the day; the significance of early trials endured and overcome provides ample food for thought.

Not far from the Kapelhoff sisters' fine mansion (left), technical buildings designed primarily for housing a cement fermenting vat (above) have been built.

CHÂTEAU
TALBOT

Saint-Julien

More than ten years after the death in September 1993 of this estate's previous master, the imprint—better, the presence—of Jean Cordier is still palpable at Talbot. The father of the current owners, Lorraine Rustmann and Nancy Bignon, is clearly still the guiding spirit here, an honor he appears to share to some degree with another father figure, the eminently venerable High Constable Talbot—a great British military man and governor of Guyenne until his defeat at Castillon in 1453. Except for the name, however, little is known of the latter's exact relationship to the present estate.

Jean Cordier's father Georges acquired Talbot shortly after World War II. The spirit of this family, combining high standards with the generosity characteristic of people from the north of France, has indelibly marked the estate ever since. This spirit can be found almost everywhere: in the ergonomic placement of the two fermenting vats—one installed in 1989, with oak casks, the other in 1994, with stainless-steel vats—and in the exemplary, totally praisewor-

thy arrangement of the cellars. At Talbot, a continuous concern for efficiency is combined with meticulous attention to the smallest details that might almost be considered overly perfectionist. Everything is so neat and clean, it's hard not to make the obvious comparison: here we have the kind of reassuring feeling usually found only in a certain type of Swiss *pension*.

The 266 acres (108 hectares) of quality vineyards lie adjacent to those of Léoville-Poyferré and Gruaud Larose, in the heart of the Saint-Julien *appellation*. It is in these vineyards that the tension animating the entire estate is most keenly felt. Each parcel of land is individually managed to maturity, made possible by the ease of computer management, guaranteeing success for the one component on which all else rests: perfect grapes.

Everything possible is done throughout the vinification process in order to draw the most accomplished endproduct from this raw material. For example, when the grapes arrive at the winery for a final sorting, they are transferred

Unchanged since the happy era of Jean Cordier,
this lovely mansion has all the graces of a carefree holiday residence.

to machines of the same type as those used at some orchards for drying fragile fruit without causing damage. Need we also mention that this equipment is unique in the Médoc? Another example, at the end of the process: the automated, aseptic, ultrasophisticated bottling room, which resembles a laboratory.

Here modernity is combined with the subtly reassuring harmony of ancient stone. This subtle alchemy is the spice animating a lively estate run with true passion for the task. "To be and to remain the proprietor of a vineyard," wrote another Cordier—Désiré—at the turn of the twentieth century, "one must be gifted with a genuine aristocratic attitude placed at the service of the estate and the wine. One must sacrifice everything to it, starting with the desire for financial gain. In a way, owning a vineyard is like being in love." When all is said in done, "being in love" is the only thing that counts—obviously. This effort, the straining for perfection, and, at the same time, the friendly and enthusiastic atmosphere manifest at Talbot, all bear the mark of a hidden wellspring so familiar it is taken for granted. The wellspring of love.

Cosseted interiors, impeccable cellars, an outstanding wine—
the inseparable components of a particular attitude to the world.

CHÂTEAU
BRANAIRE-DUCRU

Saint-Julien

When you arrive at Château Branaire-Ducru, you are handed a brochure describing the estate. So far, so ordinary. But take a second look at the brochure. It is quite different from those handed out at the other great Médoc estates. Château Branaire-Ducru's brochure is rather like the estate itself, which prides itself on its up-to-the-minute technology. The owners have obviously taken as much care with the brochure as they do with their wines: it is carefully written and beautifully printed. Such perfectionism is typical of everything Patrick Maroteaux sets his mind to. He has been running the estate for around fifteen years now. He has always had a passion for fine wine. In 1988, he set about persuading his in-laws, who had made their fortune in the sugar industry, to invest in the estate. Although the family had no background in winemaking, it proved an inspired move. Patrick has succeeded in stamping his own personality on this Fourth Growth *Cru Classé*. His approach to winemaking is so clearly laid out in the brochure that it is tempting simply to quote from it wholesale.

In the brochure, Patrick begins by explaining the characteristics of the great wines of the *appellation*, which all share, to a greater or lesser extent, "the complexity and intelligence of a pleasure shared, with … the even greater virtue of balance." I couldn't have put it better myself. The estate is situated on a magnificent outcrop on the plateau of Saint-Julien-Beychevelle, facing the river. It is ideally sized, with some hundred and twenty-five acres (fifty hectares) of vines currently in use. In other words, "Château Branaire-Ducru had all the makings of a great wine. It just needed someone to turn the potential into reality." Patrick was particularly fortunate in that the vines were just the right age. "Men and vines have much in common, including the question of age. Both are at their finest at around thirty-five years of age. Earlier, they are too young to express their full personality. Twenty years later, maturity all too often gives way to a hint of authoritarianism."

Patrick Maroteaux is particularly proud of having overseen the immense task of renovating the fermentation cellar.

*The magnificent central staircase still boasts
its Directoire period ornamentation.*

This is doubtless where his perfectionism has made the greatest mark. The complete overhaul of the cellar was one of the first tasks he set himself on acquiring the estate in 1988. "It takes more than small-scale projects to satisfy burning ambition," he smiles, before pointing out that, while the cellar is now full of high-tech machinery automatically checking every aspect of the winemaking process, he is perfectly aware that this is not in itself a guarantee of a fine wine. Of course he knows that what makes all the difference is the human touch. It takes long years of experience to know exactly how to make the most of an estate's potential.

It would be a shame to leave Château Branaire-Ducru without a visit to the delightful charterhouse. It is a charmingly unpretentious, simple building, where symmetry and unity of style are married in splendidly harmonious architecture. Patrick draws my attention to the fact that although the building was designed during the Directoire period, it bears a remarkable resemblance to the Palladian villas of sixteenth-century Italy. It is clear that Patrick has acquired a deep love for, and understanding of, these lands—the absolute prerequisite for coaxing peerless wines from the stony soil of the Bordeaux region.

The ultramodern installations of the brand-new winery (center) contrast with the classic charms of the old mansion (facing page and top).

CHÂTEAU
DUHART-MILON

Pauillac

The Rothschilds acquired the Duhart-Milon estate next to their Lafite vineyards in 1962. The property had been in the hands of the Castéja family for over a century, but they had sold it twenty-five years before and since then it had changed hands five times. None of the previous owners had been in a position to give the land the time and attention it needed to bring it up to modern standards. Of the 273 acres (110 hectares) of the property, fewer than 20 were planted with vines.

The Rothschilds were determined to restore the estate to the glory it had once known. They started a major renovation program, draining the land, replanting the vines one by one, uprooting a number of plants, tearing out the acres of overgrown Petit Verdot vines and selecting new varieties, reshaping the vineyards, building new wine cellars to cope with the vastly increased yield, and installing state-of-the-art fermentation cellars. In just twenty-five years, the vineyards saved by the Rothschilds increased from about a hundred acres (forty hectares) to over a hundred and seventy (seventy hectares).

There is some truth in the claim that the Rothschilds saw the lands of the Duhart-Milon estate as somehow their due. The property lies along the western side of the Château Lafite-Rothschild estate and it simply made sense for the same team to try and implement the same methods that had proved so successful for the Château Lafite-Rothschild vineyards. The new Château Duhart-Milon wines quickly reached a peak of excellence that would have taken much longer without these methods. Château Duhart-Milon was soon hailed by winelovers everywhere as a superb example of the best Pauillac wines. Distinguished, balanced, and full of finesse—some might even be tempted to call this Fourth Growth wine a little too purified, except for its surprising, underlying hint of sap.

The origin of the name Milon is something of a mystery. It was already in use in the early eighteenth century when the Marquis de Ségur, Seigneur de Lafite, known as the "Prince of Vines," sold the wine as an additional source of income. It seems that Duhart was the name of an

These recently constructed winery buildings reflect a massive investment on the part of the Rothschilds,
who have owned the estate since the early 1960s.

eighteenth-century pirate or corsair who stole a fortune before settling on the banks of the Gironde for a perhaps undeserved retirement. Until the middle of the twentieth century the estuary town of Pauillac boasted a pirate's house that now features on Château Duhart-Milon labels.

In the interwar years, the Castéja family seriously considered building a château worthy of a *grand cru classé* on the land. They got as far as planting a copse of oak trees near the chosen site, but the château itself was never built. Nowadays, the trees are fully grown. In their shade, coopers make casks for the Rothschild estates wines. The setting inspired a book by the novelist Claude Fischler, entitled *Balises de l'imaginaire*.

Some might say that the ghostly presence of a château that was never built is the most fitting emblem of a great wine that most wine lovers can only dream of tasting. Yet although the estate does not possess a château, it can boast of having become one of the great Médoc vineyards since the Rothschilds took it under their wing. Château Duhart-Milon has a long and rich history. Thanks to the ceaseless efforts of three generations of the Rothschild family, it once again deserves its classification as the only Fourth Growth vineyard in the Pauillac appellation.

The Rothschilds' emblematic yellow-and-blue colors proudly adorn the cement vats (left). The family's personal touch is also exhibited more subtly in these old, half-open doors leading into the majestic and impeccable cellars (above, center). We might note in passing, on the bottom of this cask (above, left), a reference identifying the parcel of land the grapes were grown on.

CHÂTEAU
POUGET

Margaux

In 2006 Lucien Guillemet will be celebrating the centenary of the day his family acquired Pouget. Others consider this occasion something to boast about, but boasting is not the style of our philosopher-vintner—a man steeped in the foundations of wisdom and clear thinking. Moreover, Guillemet's thirteen years as technical director at Giscours doubtless taught him some things perhaps not explicitly transmitted by the ancestral faith. Among them: humility in response to natural phenomena, and modesty in response to human ones. "Nature's whims are a constant throughout life," he explains, "and it's harder to change human beings than some might think. Something you can do, over the short term, is to modify vinification and blending. And, over the long term, you can also work with different rootstocks and growing methods."

Guillemet is clearly not the man to fix something that's not broken. "First-class wines existed before we came along," he points out, "and the vintner's job is to follow their lead. It's different with second-class wines, which can definitely be made more interesting." Especially, we might

add, in the case of Pouget, by far the most classic—most traditional, as it were—of the two *grands crus* produced on the Guillemet estate. The other, Boyd-Cantenac, has a velvety lightness more consistent with current tastes.

The estate's owner agrees. "With Pouget," he says, "we're definitely on familiar ground: wines with a stronger tannin content, among other properties. I'd be lying if I told you I had nothing to do with the distinction. Actually, instead of masking the tannin, I try—just a little—to emphasize it." As if to justify what he's just said, this passionately committed but cautious vintner adds, "When you get right down to it, people produce the kind of wine they like themselves, and the wine I like, when all's said and done, is a wine that's a pleasure to drink."

But aren't all wines supposed to be a pleasure to drink Lucien Guillemet's eyes gleam slyly. "The thing that counts," he answers, "is that once the bottle has been emptied into the glasses, the glasses will be emptied in their turn. With some of the greatest wines, you can see for yourself this doesn't always happen." The implication: some

Meticulous attention to the vineyard remains
the primary condition for excellence.

great vintages are so carefully calibrated to please professional critics, they can discourage ordinary drinkers, and actually put them off.

Nothing like this happens with Pouget, a wine designed to provide basic satisfaction to its extremely loyal consumers. Unlike Boyd-Cantenac, sold direct as a vintage wine, Pouget is marketed through two dealers who distribute it continuously. One of them distributes it in France (a point too rarely mentioned), the other in Northern Europe, mainly to the Benelux countries and Denmark. These customers are not particularly interested in gold medals and ratings. Apart from the slight differences that are bound to occur from year to year, they just want their favorite wine to be consistent, to exhibit the same qualities they liked at first taste and will always like, as long as they remain more or less in evidence.

This magnificent soil was already being fully exploited in the nineteenth and twentieth centuries (left), as demonstrated by this stone medallion (above, right) and this "Victory" vintage bottle (above, left).

CHÂTEAU
LA TOUR CARNET

Haut-Médoc

Let places speak for themselves. Observe them objectively and try to understand how they work. Learn about their history, seeking keys to the present in the traces that survive from the past. Lastly, abandon oneself completely to their pervading spirit, let oneself be lulled and even entranced by it. It is true, of course, that this method is easier to follow in a place that is lovely, impressive, expressive. La Tour Carnet is all of this and more. The overall appearance of the place is literally too wonderful for words.

Geographically, this fiefdom is located half-way between Bordeaux and La Pointe-de-Grave. In other words, it stands at the hub of a strategic trade route that in the past had to be defended at all costs. And so the price for erecting ruinously expensive fortifications was paid. During the endless conflict between the French and the English for mastery of Guyenne, the local feudal lords—and particularly those of the Foix dynasty—demonstrated greater fealty to the lions of England than to the lily of France. They needed the protection of their fortifications, which had been built long

before the Hundred Years' War. The stately donjon rising above the estate, known in the Middle Ages as the Tour Saint-Laurent, had been repelling would-be invaders with its powerful defensive structures since 1120—a fact noted on the great wine's labels—preceding by a century the first vineyards planted in the land around it.

Geologically, the promontory of La Tour Carnet is a local curiosity. This jagged rock-face overlooking the vineyard from a height of over sixty feet (nineteen meters) is notable for the fact—considered miraculous by vintners—that it rests on a base of high chalk-content clay soil covered with fine Garonne and Pyrenees gravel. It thus comes as no surprise to learn that this vineyard spearheaded the production of top-quality wines in the area. Its owners were able to charge premium prices for its production as far back as the fifteenth century. It's commonly recognized that the great La Tour Carnet wine was already indisputably one of the most highly prized, several centuries before the 1855 rankings were established.

The fortified donjon visible from afar would make an ideal setting
for a sound-and-light show on the Hundred Years' War.

Somewhat paradoxically, the defensive nature of this fortified position encourages a particularly agreeable lifestyle. The rugged terrain and shady woods around the château, the romantic moat and charming sixteenth- and seventeenth-century houses clustered behind an eighteenth-century wrought-iron gate—all of this bears out the fulsome praise expressed by eminent visitors in the past: Montaigne and La Boétie, of course, whose ghosts still roam here, but also a family drawn from the Swedish aristocracy, the Luetkens, who protected the estate from the excesses of the French Revolution.

In 2000—might this round number be symbolic?—La Tour Carnet was taken in hand by Bernard Magrez, and his mark is perceptible in every sip of the wine. Not only did the new owner brilliantly restore the manor house, he also immediately set out to improve the quality of the vineyards. The installation of modern equipment has been instrumental in returning his great wine to its former excellence. Specifically, eighteen recently acquired wooden casks holding exactly 1,848 gallons (seventy hectoliters) each should facilitate meticulous monitoring of the wine according to the individual parcels of land on which the grapes were grown.

A keen sense of drama is another aspect of the new system. In the long cellar some fourteen hundred casks—half of them new—have been arranged in tiers on either side of a central nave. This "wine amphitheater" is surely one of the most impressive sights in any cellar.

This admirable mansion house (facing page) is the best symbol a wine-growing estate could have. Everything contributes to its luxury, from the façades to the salon anterooms, which rival the cask cellar in majesty.

CHÂTEAU
LAFON-ROCHET

Saint-Estèphe

When Alfred and Michel Tesseron's father Guy acquired Lafon-Rochet in May 1960, he immediately infused it with the calm assurance of a man born and bred among the vineyards of Cognac. At the time, everyone agreed that the property was in a state of advanced decrepitude. The most visible sign of this abandon was the château, then a virtual ruin. Restoration would have been extremely costly, the results far from assured. The new owner therefore decided simply to raze what remained of the existing walls. Starting with a clean slate, he set about constructing a château in the purest eighteenth-century style, from the ground up. Nothing like this had ever before been done in the Bordeaux region, and probably nothing like it will ever be done again; nevertheless, it is a telling illustration of what a little daring can accomplish, in our own time, to reweave the fabric connecting us to the great and emblematic Médoc châteaux of the past.

The architect commissioned for the project understood what was wanted, and soon Lafon-Rochet again boasted a château of classic design, though of ultramodern construction, affording the great wine produced on the surrounding land a setting at last worthy of its quality and rank. Michel Tesseron, who has taken over here from his father just as his brother Alfred has done at Pontet-Canet, decided to add a distinctive finishing touch to the project: he had the outside walls of the château painted a shade of bright sunshine yellow inspired by the Russian palaces of Potemkin's time. This vivid, eye-catching color is now the estate's signature. It appears on the wine's labels and was also used for painting the new winery.

The winery buildings are also relatively recent additions to the estate, and to say that Michel Tesseron exerted a special effort to make them both efficient and visually appealing would be an understatement. "It doesn't cost any more to make things look nice," he explains. To cite just one example, the fermentation rooms have been given theatrical lighting. In the first-year cellar, imposing pink columns with flared tops—somewhat reminiscent of the Minoan

The new château has struck a bright note in the Saint-Estèphe vineyard
ever since Michel Tesseron had the façades painted yellow.

palaces at Knossos—are equipped with a peripheral sprinkler system that, when necessary, sprays them with a thin film of water. The visual impact of this procedure is striking, and also serves an important purpose by humidifying the air inside the cellar.

Make no mistake, however: devices such as this are merely minor adjustments to the essential core operations, which are of course wholly focused on the overwhelming assets of the vineyard. This 110 acre (45 hectare) stretch of land, long recognized and envied for its quality, lies in the Saint-Estèphe area bordering Pauillac, nestled between the vineyards of its prestigious neighbors Cos d'Estournel, visible just beyond the path, and Lafite-Rothschild. Michel Tesseron's goal is to extract everything possible from this land's potential, drawing on its vital substance year after

year. Comparing himself to a great chef producing only a single dish per year, he proclaims that his intention is to make this "dish" truly exceptional. With poetic intensity, he reiterates his conviction that, "Winemakers owe everything to nature—to the soil, the rootstock, the weather—and this makes them humble. So does their own passion, which has burned within them since birth." As he speaks, listeners can almost hear that passion throbbing. Drawing on a deep sense of satisfaction, he concludes, "That's what makes us happy."

Apart from the totally modern winery (left),
the estate also boasts more ancient charms,
such as those of the little chapel, the horseshoe steps,
and this engraved curbstone (above).

CHÂTEAU
BEYCHEVELLE

Saint-Julien

The Beychevelle château has frequently been referred to as the "Versailles of the Médoc," but it would be more accurate to call it a "Grand Trianon" in the Bordeaux style. Such a description by no means suggests a step down; on the contrary, it underscores the harmonious grandeur projected by this residence and the charm inherent in its monumentality. Just like Mansart's masterpiece, the Trianon, the main body of the edifice is composed of a long upper story built on a solid foundation and crowned with Italian-style rooftops surrounded by balustrades. Two extensive wings forming elbows, as it were, are interrupted at intervals by projecting structures roofed with slate. Most of the basic architectural design, although inevitably remodeled during the nineteenth and twentieth centuries, dates from the middle of the eighteenth century, when the Marquis de Brassier rebuilt the major portion of the château in magnificent style.

Visitors enter through a courtyard worthy of the finest residences; but it is the other façade, on the garden side, that has the most stunning surprises in store. From terraces overlooking manicured French gardens, the gaze travels past a series of immaculate flower beds to the nearby marshes along the river. Here is an amazing vista of which the eyes never tire, certainly one of the finest views of the Gironde to be had anywhere in the Médoc. It naturally evokes the thought that an estate offering such a unique feast for the eyes must also produce a great wine distinct from all others. Beychevelle is clearly doomed to greatness—both literally and figuratively.

It is a point of honor at all noble houses to revere the memory of illustrious former occupants. Here, given pride of place above the neo-Renaissance mantel in one of a series of formal salons, hangs a portrait of the flamboyant Duc d'Epernon, a favorite of Henri III and then of Marie de Médicis, and lord of Beychevelle during his governorship of Guyenne. Legend has it that when ships plying the Gironde passed his fiefdom, they demonstrated their fealty by lowering their sails. This custom is said to form the origin of the

The pilasters adorned with seventeenth-century firepots in the forecourt
introduce visitors to an architecture unique in the Médoc region.

estate's name: "Beychevelle," from *baisse-voile*, meaning "lowered sails."

Nearer our own time, the estate's fortunes were guided for almost a century, from 1890 to 1989, by the Achille-Fould family, descendants of the great minister and banker under Napoleon III. In 1970 the contemporary heir of this dynasty, Aymar Achille-Fould, sought invaluable assistance from the famous Dr. Peynaud. Together the two men decided to make the criteria governing rootstock selection more stringent, and thus, logically, to improve the quality of this great wine. Their theory was borne out in practice, and is still followed today by Dr. Peynaud's successors, Pascal Ribéreau-Gayon and Jacques Boissenot. A shareholder since 1984, the GMF group purchased a majority stake in 1986 when Aymar Achille-Fould died, and in 1988 joined with the Japanese Suntory group in creating the Société des Grands Millésimes de France, the current owner.

The thumbnail sketches in this volume are intended to highlight the points of interest characterizing each estate.

In the case of Beychevelle, we might mention the fact, for those who don't know it already, that the estate has long possessed its own farm and raises its own cattle. These animals supply all the natural manure required in the vineyards. But the estate's enduring involvement in numerous prestigious civic projects of more than purely local interest is no doubt more fascinating. After instituting a sort of Villa Medici in Aquitaine, and then welcoming the screen-writing workshops of the Associaton Equinox headed by Jeanne Moreau, Beychevelle continues to support numerous cultural events, notably outstanding musical events. "This château is a private house no longer," say those who come here; "its doors are now wide open to every wine lover in the world."

In the time of the Duc d'Epernon (above, center),
the façades on the river side had not yet by any means
attained the breadth they acquired in the seventeenth,
eighteenth, and nineteenth centuries (left).

CHÂTEAU
PRIEURÉ-LICHINE

Margaux

Some places seem destined for a fate apart. Like those men and women who appear to be accompanied by a lucky star throughout their lives, certain estates are impervious to the blows of fate and endlessly reborn from their ashes. Château Prieuré-Lichine is one of these: it has survived revolutionary requisitions, vineyard diseases, and the disappearance of a great benefactor, emerging strengthened and renewed from each successive ordeal.

Little is now known about the Cantenac priory founded in the sixteenth century by monks from the Abbey of Vertheuil; an investigation of its history would provide a wonderful thesis topic for students interested in the Médoc. What we do know, at least, is that the wine produced in those days by the monks had a very good reputation and that the surplus they sold on the market was a benchmark for all the region's wines. In other words, the priory had established its reputation for producing fine wine long before it was acquired by the state—at which point its sole raison d'être became its vineyards.

The vicissitudes of Château Le Prieuré—the estate's name at the time of the 1855 rankings—would make a fascinating story. However, this story is eclipsed by the one beginning in 1951, the year the property was acquired by a man who surely must have been the most flamboyant individual ever connected with the priory: Alexis Lichine. Born in the United States to Russian émigré parents, this youthful wine dealer conceived his passion for *grand cru* wines early in life. It was he who set out to raise wine in the public imagination to the same level as other universally recognized cultural artifacts such as painting and music. Dubbed the "Pope of Wine" by the New York press, this master of modernity—as scintillating as Vladimir Nabokov and grandiloquent as Sacha Guitry—not only rallied his American compatriots to the cause of French wine but revealed to the French themselves (starting with the denizens of the Bordeaux region) the terrific potential of their oenological treasures.

In 1953 Château Prieuré-Cantenac was officially renamed Prieuré-Lichine. Through subsequent exchanges

This unusual wall, decorated with metal fire-backs,
gives some idea of Alexis Lichine's taste.

and even more numerous purchases of land ranked among the three *premiers crus*, Alexis Lichine succeeded in endowing his property with a vineyard that was vast overall, although split into smaller parcels. Over a span of three decades the total area was increased from twenty-seven acres (eleven hectares) to one hundred and fifty acres (over sixty hectares). Lichine was everywhere at once. His experience as a vintner and his intimate knowledge of vinification methods were astounding, and they swiftly raised the reputation of the "new" *grand cru* high above its initial ranking. Lichine's eloquence, sense of public relations, and hospitality in the grand manner did the rest; wine critics were soon eating out of his hand.

But every coin has its reverse side. When Alexis Lichine departed from the scene in 1989—he was buried on one of the loveliest sections of the property, not far from the railroad line—the sudden void left by his absence augured ill for the future. Nevertheless, his son Sacha Lichine courageously gathered up the reins of the estate, adopting a high-yield policy much criticized at the time but which, all things considered, was defensible. Sacha sold the jewel of his

father's holdings ten years later to the Ballande group. Although relatively unfamiliar with the Médoc world, the group proved to have skills (the lucky star was still shining over Prieuré-Lichine) that led to yet another renaissance.

The fresh team placed in charge of the property immediately abandoned the idea of high yield and quick profits in order to concentrate on the vineyard's strong underlying potential. In this, they returned to a particular idea of excellence and restored credibility to Prieuré-Lichine. New management directives specified that the traditional breeding, elegance, and subtle complexity of this great wine should be restored. The first priority was to modify vinification methods; the second to give careful attention to the "raw material," that is, the vines themselves. This was the price that had to be paid to return Prieuré-Lichine to its position as the "navel" or centerpiece of the Margaux *appellation*.

The priory has clearly lost none of its charm, nor the garden any of its stunning visual impact. The cask cellar features rather spectacular blue support-columns (left).

CHÂTEAU
MARQUIS DE TERME

Margaux

In the dark years following the 1929 Wall Street crash and the ensuing global economic crisis, many Bordeaux estates changed hands while others were carved up for sale to different buyers. This was the fate that befell the Marquis de Terme estate, which belonged to the Feuillerats until 1935, when it was sold to the Sénéclauze family. The Sénéclauze family had been living for many years in the city of Oran in Algeria—in those days still a French colony— and had built up an enviable reputation as importers of fine Algerian wines. This was not perhaps the ideal background for making the best of the Médoc *terroir*: the climate was much less sunny and the soil infinitely more complex than in Algeria. Pierre Sénéclauze, like his three sons who took over the estate in later years, avoided the pitfall of thinking he could transfer the lessons learned in Algeria wholesale. Instead, he set a general direction he wanted the vineyard to go in, and delegated the day-to-day running of the estate to a highly experienced local man.

Since then, the running of the Marquis de Terme estate has been in the hands of just two men. Their remarkably long period of service speaks volumes about their competence and the confidence the Sénéclauzes had in their abilities. Pierre Sénéclauze hired Alexandre Tolo first of all. He retired in 1974 and handed the reins over to Jean-Pierre Hugon, a well-known face in the Médoc region. Jean-Pierre is himself the son of a winemaker. His language is the language of the earth and the seasons. Casting his mind back to his early days in charge, he recalls the errors of the early days with indulgence and a hint of nostalgia. "In the early 1970s," he says, "Our main objective was just to increase the yield. Compared to what we're doing today, it could hardly be called good work. We were dealing with different grape varieties all growing on the same plots, while the wine cellar was terribly impractical and not exactly spotlessly clean. The fermentation cellar was not up to the task, and some of the casks were over twenty years old!" he adds with a chuckle.

This balcony, overlooking a tree-shaded park, gives some idea of the serenity
reigning in the mansion's immediate surroundings.

Yet that did not prevent the team from producing some memorable wines, such as the 1975 vintage.

However, there was no escaping the fact that serious improvements needed to be made to every step of the wine-making process if Marquis de Terme were to reach its full potential. "You could call the work of the past twenty-five years a resurrection," Jean-Pierre Hugon says. He proudly lists all the changes he and his team have patiently put in place, season after season—adding thirty acres (twelve hectares) of vines over twenty-five years, improving the choice of grape varieties, renovating the fermentation cellar and replacing the old concrete vat with a stainless-steel one, building a new cellar for aging the casks of wine in the 1980s, as well as new facilities for packaging and storage. He is also proud of the way he has stood firm with other independent wine merchants in their dealings with the large supermarket chains.

But this does not mean that the managers of the Marquis de Terme estate follow technology blindly. They have always thought carefully about what advantages such innovations will bring them. For important issues such as cloning grape varieties or corking the wines in carefully modified atmospheric conditions, the question is debated long and hard before any decision is made. The estate manager is careful never to impose his view, and makes a point of listening to the opinions of everyone involved in the winemaking process.

Jean-Pierre Hugon loves his work. His only grumble is the never-ending stream of paperwork covering everything from health and safety issues to waste disposal. He resents having to spend precious hours inside at his desk when he could be putting them to better use out in the vineyards, doing the job he was hired to do: producing a wine that is worthy of the Marquis de Terme *terroir* and that upholds the *appellation* it has the honor to belong to.

The classical elegance of a charterhouse in the heart of the vineyards (bottom). A traditional aging cellar, with part of its solid frame built underground (center). The estate's wine label has not changed for many years. The coat of arms on the chimney breast dates back centuries (facing page). The concrete vats covered in earthenware tiles are rather unusual (top).

Château Pontet-Canet

Château Batailley

Château Haut-Batailley

Château Grand-Puy-Lacoste

Château Grand-Puy Ducasse

Château Lynch-Bages

Château Lynch-Moussas

Château Dauzac

Château d'Armailhac

Château du Tertre

Château Haut-Bages Libéral

Château Pédesclaux

Château Belgrave

Château Camensac

Château Cos Labory

Château Clerc Milon

Château Croizet-Bages

Château Cantemerle

CHÂTEAU
PONTET-CANET

Pauillac

The mild, golden evening light so often seen in the Pauillac region gleams on the vineyard of Pontet-Canet, almost two hundred acres (eighty hectares) of evenly spaced rows bordering the estate of its prestigious neighbor, Mouton Rothschild. The eye wanders over a rolling landscape to the endless hills beyond. Shadows lengthen on the château's slender promontory overlooking the distant river, and in the harmoniously proportioned courtyards around the wineries darkness gathers. The week is ending. Alfred Tesseron, wearing boots and a hat, makes a final tour of inspection. His eyes gleam with justifiable pride as, one by one, he closes the iron curtains of his "shop" behind him. The all-encompassing glance he casts over his domain expresses his satisfaction with a job well done.

It's worthy of note, in fact, that the substantial sums invested over a span of just a few years have made possible the total renovation of an estate originally roused from its somnolence by Tesseron's father. Since then, the son and his team have deployed rational analysis and extensive expertise

in the major task of improving the methods used to harvest and process grapes. One of their innovations, for example, is the use of plastic containers designed specifically to facilitate grape handling and transport. Sorting takes place in a purpose-built upper-floor room that is large, well lit, and perfectly ergonomic. Flexibility and maximum yield are ensured by sending the sorted batches of grapes, "as pure and glistening as caviar," by conveyor to one of three different vats—wooden, cement, or stainless steel. The quality of the equipment and genuine beauty of the immense storage cellars add the finishing touch to a winery recently completed by the addition of a third all-new courtyard surrounded by buildings for storage and processing.

Pontet-Canet has perhaps taken longer than other vineyards to adopt modern methods, but the Tesserons have never acted rashly. Wryly, Alfred recalls his father's explosive reaction to the first "green harvests" pioneered here in 1994. Tesseron Senior, an excellent vintner of the old school who had spent years increasing the property's yield, balked at the

Twin staircases lead from the winery to the upper-story room
where harvested grapes are collected.

frivolous "wasting" of entire bunches of grapes. He was not won over until the great wine produced according to the new methods received unanimous praise from enthusiastic critics.

It's true enough that the days when the Blue Train and the Compagnie des Wagons Lits listed Pontet-Canet on their menus are long gone—but the prestige of this fifth *cru de première classe* has never been higher than it is today. The new, disciplined management of the estate is obviously the reason. A discipline that is effective, but discreet. "In my view," says Alfred Tesseron, "the crucial factor, and one I never lose sight of, is the 'good life' aspect of our wines' image." The château's hospitable warmth, imposing polished columns, impressive wrought-iron banisters, and beautiful tiled mantelpieces bear out its owner's words.

The salons are empty now, as night falls, but it's easy to imagine them filled with a host of convivial wine lovers linked to the local soil and possessing a unique expertise, wine lovers both erudite and open to new ideas, aware of history but devoid of the sterile pedantry exhibited by some experts. In short, guests one would rejoice at seeing, in the words of Jacques Prévert, "intoxicated with French history and Pontet-Canet."

This comfortable mansion contains a fine staircase and inviting salons, enhanced by wooden columns.

241

CHÂTEAU
BATAILLEY

Pauillac

We pass through an elegant hall that is straight out of a Serebryakov watercolor into a comfortable drawing-room full of solid nineteenth-century furniture. The scent of wax polish hangs in the air like homage to the virtues of domesticity. Next is a library with shelves of books floor to ceiling, with something of the atmosphere of a well-stocked wine cellar. A few rare editions with magnificent bindings are on display. Finally, we come to the dining room, typical of the region, where succulent dishes are served in the finest porcelain accompanied by carefully selected vintages served in crystal goblets. It is a shame that such a magnificent home should be open to just a few select visitors under the discretion of Madame Castéja, *née* Borie, the current manager's mother. The building was formerly a charterhouse, and is one of the few in the Bordeaux region to have maintained the family traditions that for two and a half centuries have given the Médoc region such an enviable reputation for good living.

The current manager, Philippe Castéja, is as discreet as his mother in his own way. He is a master of understatement, beginning our guided visit by telling us, "We have some rather fine buildings," before showing us into one of the most splendid wine cellars I have ever seen. He generally prefers to let the many assets of his estate speak for themselves. The Batailley estate was split off from a larger estate in 1942. This is clearly the better half. So modest is Philippe Castéja that he barely mentions that the grounds were laid out by Barillet-Deschamps, landscape gardener to Napoleon III and the Empress Eugenie, no less. He also lets slip in passing that the barn, with its vaguely familiar-looking elegant metal structure, was used during the Universal Exhibition in 1889 to store the girders used to build the Eiffel Tower.

Philippe's father, Emile shares the frank common sense one finds in many of the great winegrowers of his generation. He enjoys sharing his memories of a not-so-distant past when the Médoc had lost much of its former prestige and had yet to benefit from the commercial upturn of the 1980s. He talks freely of the days when winegrowers had to struggle to make the best of difficult conditions and when

The French and Austrian flags fly side by side at the entrance to the house,
since the estate's owner is the Austrian consul in Bordeaux.

many suffered hardship. He faultlessly recalls the weather conditions in various years noted for the outstanding quality of the vintage—and other years when the results were less impressive. The year 1961, when he took over from Marcel Borie, had perfect weather for grapes. In 1974, the weather was awful, and the 1974 vintage is indeed distinctly average.

Today, Philippe Castéja manages the Batailley estate with the tact and efficiency that have made him such an excellent president of the *Conseil des Grands Crus Classés*. He has a special gift for making the best of what he is given while avoiding the less positive aspects. He is perfectly at ease with the codes and rituals of a world where the least *faux pas* is severely frowned upon. In a word, he has the soul of a diplomat (although it is his father who holds the position of honorary consul for Austria). These personal qualities have been of immense benefit to the estate. Château Batailley is today widely acknowledged to be one of the finest of all Pauillac wines.

In the land of Montaigne and Montesquieu, one expects to find well-stocked libraries, but in vain: the library at Batailley is actually something of a rarity (facing page). This little Bacchus (center) recalls the Perkeo of Heidelberg; its tutelary presence is intended to confer prosperity on the fine courtyards, the remarkable cellar, and the Castéjas' house.

CHÂTEAU
HAUT-BATAILLEY

Pauillac

Here is an estate that owes its ultracontemporary renaissance to the very personal, if perfectly laudable, motives of its owner. "During the 1940s," explains François-Xavier Borie today, "my grandfather felt the need to have a *grand cru* vineyard all his own—a piece of land on which he would be free to make all the decisions just as he liked. At the time he was a partner, with my great-uncle, in the Borie Frères wine dealership. He had to sell a percentage of his share in order to acquire Haut-Batailley, which he considered ideal for his purposes, and it was he who installed the facilities indispensable for the production of a great wine. He restored and enlarged the existing buildings—those large Basque-style structures you can still see today—and converted them into an efficient winery."

The most striking aspect of the Haut-Batailley setting is also the least representative and most occasional, as it were, imaginable. This is the romantic, slightly rickety, slightly frail white tower that the Averous sisters—who expressed the depth of their piety through frequent pilgrimages to Lourdes—constructed on the estate's border with Lynch-Bages. It's named the "Asp Tower," a reference to the satanic serpent, crushed underfoot by the Virgin Mary to symbolize the triumph of Good over Evil.

The tower apart, however, Haut-Batailley suffers rather strongly from a relative lack of identity—as even François-Xavier Borie is quick to recognize. Furthermore, it is clear that in the family's overall strategy for the estates it owns, this one does not really play a leading role. In short, let's just say that the primary function of the 100,000 bottles or so produced here annually is to "hold their ground"—simply to occupy a market position that would otherwise be overrun by competitors.

This doesn't mean that the great Haut-Batailley wine isn't worthy of its 1855 ranking. On the contrary, it easily justifies the position it holds. One might only note that it's a little more delicate, a little more feminine than the classic Pauillac. Its mellower, more accessible style and its obvious finesse tend to place it apart, in a somewhat special category of an *appellation* of which it is atypical. However, it is precisely this flexible accessibility that has allowed Haut-Batailley to carve out an enviable niche for itself on the wine lists of leading restaurants, where it can be relied on to flatter the palates of connoisseurs.

The Virgin on the roof of the Asp Tower, visible from the far-distant vineyard,
reflects the demonstrative piety of the Averous sisters.

These outbuildings area synthesis of different styles from the South-West, with a touch of influence from the Basque region.

CHÂTEAU
GRAND-PUY-LACOSTE

Pauillac

Knoll, hillock, mound, puy—these are the topographical terms designating the protuberances rising from a relatively flat landscape that play such a decisive role in vineyard drainage and thus enhance an estate's value. The highest point, or puy, at Grand-Puy-Lacoste, for example, rises some sixty-five feet (twenty meters) to the north of the main road linking Pauillac to Saint-Laurent. Lacoste is the name of the family who owned this estate from the beginning of the eighteenth century until the end of the nineteenth, when the phylloxera epidemic struck. The name of the estate also once included that of a collateral branch, Saint-Guirons, subsequently dropped.

From 1932 until 1978 the estate was the exclusive domain of a legendary figure in the annals of Médoc wine, Raymond Dupin. A bon vivant and lord of the manor in the old-school mode, Ecole Polytechnique graduate Dupin was president of the Union des Crus Classés du Médoc and an epicurean in the noblest, most philosophical sense of the term. Descended from a line of attorneys practicing in the Landes region, he saw his own role as that of an orchestra conductor—a guiding spirit, as it were. On the practical side, he willingly delegated the estate's management to "proxies" (as he called them). An invitation to this connoisseur's table amounted to official recognition of membership in the exclusive world of great châteaux, and provided an edifying glimpse—or so people say—of how elegant and refined hedonism at its best can be.

The aging Dupin was apparently obsessed for years with the problem of finding the right people to carry on his work. He solved this knotty problem by deciding to pass the torch on to Jean-Eugène Borie and Borie's son François-Xavier—two men who had amply proved their worth, at Ducru-Beaucaillou in particular. The necessary arrangements were made in the course of two memorable luncheon parties that smoothed the way for the transaction. Subsequent events were to bear out the wisdom of Dupin's final choice: the Bories went on to position Grand-Puy-Lacoste to enable it to reap maximum benefit from the

The ghost of famed Raymond Dupin still hovers over the comfortable ground-floor salons.

expansion of the 1980s. Better yet, starting in the early years of the following decade, this great wine regained a preeminence that now ranks it, according to the experts, higher than when it was first classified in 1855.

The years passed. Working with his father since 1978, François-Xavier this year began devoting his efforts essentially to Grand-Puy-Lacoste while also becoming involved in the family's other estates. With shrewd foresight, this elder brother—now worrying about his own legacy—decided to pass the reins of the Saint-Julien estate to his brother and sister and settle permanently at Grand-Puy-Lacoste. He had always felt at home on the familiar estate, a safe haven where new family members are regularly baptized in the chapel. Thus did the estate's former manager find himself as happy "as a fish in water," settling in as if he'd never been away. He knows, of course, that he can count on the support of an entire team deeply attached to family tradition.

Against this supportive background, major new renovation projects have been undertaken in order to modernize the production facilities. In the Borie family, no one ever forgets that the key to all of this is still the wine—a product more apt to free the human spirit than to constrain it. "Above a certain level of quality," explains the worthy successor of the old Ecole Polytechnique graduate, "wine becomes a kind of language. A universal language, a little like music or sports. It really makes me happy to see that my children understand this. They realize that wine is most of all an extraordinary means of communication—an amazing opening onto the world."

While we speak, a servant unobtrusively crosses the salon. She's almost as at home here as she would be in her own house. This is because she was once employed by the legendary Monsieur Dupin, and knew him well. But her loyalty to the great man's memory in no way detracts from her affection for the family today. The message we can read in this woman's eyes is living proof of a deep attachment that corporate vineyard owners, even the best in the world, will never inspire.

The manor, surrounded by its outbuildings (facing page), has preserved all the attributes of a fine house: cellar, stone trophies, antique furnishings—and even a pond with swans.

CHÂTEAU
GRAND-PUY DUCASSE

Pauillac

At Pauillac, the Gironde quayside has the kind of idle, nostalgic summer-resort feeling more usually associated with small seaports. It forms a long pedestrian pathway from which a vista of boats, fishing nets, and shoreline melts into a watery backdrop lapping at the edges of Ile Philippe and composes a crisp, brightly-colored picture—one remote indeed from the earthy and sometimes austere image usually projected by the Médoc vineyards. And yet here, a step away from the *mairie* in the middle of town, stands the Médoc region's sole truly urban château: Grand-Puy Ducasse.

Needless to say, of course, the actual vineyards—unlike those of Haut-Brion—are not planted around the château. They lie several miles away, split into three separate parcels. The largest, to the west, forms a natural extension of the Grand-Puy sector; the second lies due north of Pauillac, near Pontet-Canet; the third, farther south, near Batailley, covers part of the Saint-Lambert plateau. Together they total just under a hundred and fifty acres (sixty hectares), two-thirds of which are planted with vineyards.

Does that mean that the château itself—a lovely nineteenth-century building—is simply a showcase for the estate? Not at all. The entire north wing is given over to a modern, functional winery that fills the space inside without destroying the architectural harmony of the building's façades. The château's cellars lie under the south wing. Any lingering doubts are thus put to rest: it really is here, right in the center of Pauillac, that the great Grand-Puy Ducasse wine is made.

The estate's fortunes are guided by a two-man team working under the aegis of Cordier Mestrezat, the company that acquired it in 1971. Both of these men are not only passionately attached to the Médoc region, but also exhibit an enthusiasm for Sauternes wines that bodes well for the future. They both agree on one important point: here as there, no wines have ever been produced in the past equal

Who would ever imagine that this vast cask cellar is located in the middle of a town, in the very heart of Pauillac.

to those being produced today, at the start of the twenty-first century. This said, the two men come from very different, or at least complementary, spheres. Alain Duhau, the estate's manager, is an energetic, exacting, down-to-earth man—which doesn't prevent him from standing back and waxing philosophical at times. Bernard Monteau, on the other hand, projects an image that is both less serious and more intellectual; nonetheless, he never loses sight of the concrete problems involved in the preparation of his favorite nectar. A true son of the Médoc region—every stone and stream of which he knows by heart—he's first and foremost a man of the soil. He believes that the châteaux on the great wine-growing estates are gifts of fortune in a region that otherwise—with only a few exceptions—boasts no quaint villages or important monuments.

Looking outward and seeking new markets is obviously Alain Duhau's specialty. This tireless traveler grasps his pilgrim's staff and sets off every year to visit some of the remotest spots in the world. Today, for example, he's just back from Krasnoyarsk, where he was entertained by a club of enlightened connoisseurs who, after charming him with the warmth of their welcome, surprised him with their extensive knowledge of Bordeaux wines. "It's our job to form tastes and encourage product loyalty in the most unexpected places," explains this born evangelist. "Over the long term, this is what will perhaps save us from a fate worse than death for estates like ours: becoming banal." Monsieur Duhau needn't worry. Nowadays, Grand-Puy Ducasse is anything but banal.

These elegant and discreet buildings overlooking the docks contain vast apartments, including a large reception room (facing page).

CHÂTEAU
LYNCH-BAGES

Pauillac

Located on the outskirts of Pauillac, the pretty little hamlet of Bages has for the past seven decades served as the setting for a dramatic saga: the tale of the Cazes family, which almost eclipses that of the vineyard's Irish founders, the Lynches. Members of the Cazes family, which has become a local institution, today cherish the memory of their origins as "mountain people" from the Pyrenees. During the heroic era of the industrial revolution, their remote ancestor Jean descended from his mountaintop village to seek his fortune on the plain below.

He eventually settled among the vineyards of the Médoc region, establishing his family there as if in a promised land. It so happened that Jean Cazes's little house stood next to the Pichon-Longueville estate: his tenacious younger son Jean-Charles, who married the baker's daughter, struck up a friendship with the château's owners. In the 1950s Jean-Charles's son, André, earned their genuine esteem—as an insurance agent.

In 1933, at the request of the château's then owner, the shrewd General Félix de Vial, Jean Charles was installed as tenant farmer at Lynch-Bages. The estate's wine business began to do very well, thanks to a marketing network controlled by the eminent Cruse family of distinguished wine dealers. In 1939 the Cazes family was able to buy the estate outright. This was their first step on the high road trodden by successful businessmen who also attend to their public duties.

André Cazes, obviously an enterprising man, forged valuable personal relationships and served as mayor of Pauillac for forty-two years. In the aftermath of World War II, he joined forces with a small group of neighboring estate owners to found the *Commanderie du Bontemps de Médoc*. André Cazes was a strong believer in the importance of promoting his wines in France and throughout the world, especially at a time when superb quality—remember the sublime vintages of the 1950s—was ill-served by overproduction.

The next person in line was Jean-Michel, the leading light in the fourth generation. When he took over in the 1970s the wave had long since crested, times were hard, and "modernity" was sweeping all before it. Back in those days Jean-Michel Cazes was firmly established as an engineer in the nascent field of computer science. Nevertheless, for

*Jean-Michel Caze's appreciation of vineyard traditions
is expressed in this small private museum.*

reasons only he could explain, this dynamic and visionary Parisian decided—as his ancestor Jean had done before him—to leave his "village" and settle in the Médoc. Like his grandfather Jean-Charles, Jean-Michel is a connoisseur of good food and especially of good bread (a passion of his); like his father André, he has a keen business sense and a commitment to community activism. To being rooted and making a contribution.

Heading a youthful and enthusiastic team, Jean-Michel Cazes relaunched Lynch-Bages, dusted it off, revitalized it. "Great wines in quest of the absolute" is one of his slogans, and other family holdings are benefiting from this fresh approach. So are the various businesses controlled by the family—notably Cordeillan-Bages, one of the "Relais & Châteaux," which has swiftly become one of the best local restaurants, and in Bordeaux the *Chapon Fin*, which today has regained its past splendor.

Convinced that wine belongs to that vast universe in which geography, history, culture, and the art of fine living are closely intertwined, he founded and presides over the Ecole du Bordeaux, which spreads the good word throughout the planet.

Meanwhile, the pretty little hamlet of Bages on the outskirts of Pauillac is emerging from the sleepy decline to which, here as elsewhere, the indifference of a thankless era had consigned it. Jean-Michel Cazes has acquired a number of houses and former shops in the village, and plans to open a café that will once again ring with the voices of satisfied customers seated on its terrace. He is also hoping to restore the little covered market, and has already reopened the bakery that stocks delectable babas au rhum—a specialty of his grandmother's.

*Pergolas and summer house (above) combine
harmoniously with the modern winery
and its stainless-steel vats (left).*

CHÂTEAU
LYNCH-MOUSSAS

Pauillac

Quite apart from its reputation as a fine vineyard, Lynch-Moussas has a long and impressive history as a hunting lodge for the aristocracy. In days gone by, the king of Spain and his retinue would drive up in their jalopies, blaring their horns, ready to enjoy a weekend in the country and a shooting party hunting the woodcock that are so plentiful in the dense woodlands that cover part of the estate. Nowadays, the family still organizes hunting parties several times a year, although on a much smaller scale than in its heyday. These days, the grand house on the estate is above all a family home. It has been restored from top to bottom in a style that is sober and elegant, with an occasional lighter touch such as the cheeky pointed hat on the pepper-pot turret on the roof. The atmosphere of the house can perhaps best be described as one of a quiet, aristocratic confidence in its own taste—something it shares with many fine stately homes in England. The house has been home to Monsieur and Madame Philippe Castéja for

twenty-five years. The couple have an illustrious heritage: the Castéjas have been one of the foremost families in the Bordeaux wine trade for more than three hundred years.

A certain Count Lynch was mayor of Bordeaux during the First Empire, under Napoleon. He loved this country residence, staying here often. In fact, he died in one of the bedrooms. His other country estate, Lynch-Bages, originally bordered on these lands. Although the Lynch-Moussas estate is in the very southwestern tip of the *appellation*, it is not very far from the town of Pauillac and the river. When the 1855 classification was drawn up, the estate belonged to a Spanish family, Vasquez, and was included in the Fifth Growth category. It was only in the dark days after World War I that the estate, then relatively run down, was acquired by the Castéja family.

In 1971, Emile Castéja, then managing director of the Bordeaux wine merchants Borie-Manoux, took over the thirty five hectares of the today fifty three hectares of vines

With its lofty double doors and marble columns featuring faux-stone ornaments,
the house's vestibule effortlessly asserts a noble authority.

which were encroaching upon the neighboring estate of Batailley. The vineyards had been neglected for some fifty years and were in poor condition. So Emile Castéja got down to work to bring the vineyard and its wine into line with the other estates that shared the same classification but which had forged ahead in terms of quality while Lynch-Moussas slumbered. He set about modernizing the estate, a significant undertaking which took until the present-day to bear fruit—but the finest things in life are always worth waiting for.

These days, it is Emile's son Philippe, president of the Conseil des Grands Crus, who runs the show at Lynch-Moussas. He has spared no effort in his determination to bring Lynch-Moussas up to the level of the best wines. After years of effort, his labors have now paid off. Wine critics now all agree that this *Grand Cru* now fully deserves its place in the classification once more. They particularly admire the deep color, refined bouquet, and exquisite subtlety of what has turned into an excellent Pauillac. As Philippe Castéja himself says, "Now at long last, we can see what a Château Lynch-Moussas should be like—a beautifully supple, firm wine that is wellrounded and very balanced."

Set in a charming park and bursting with life behind its inviting façade (left), the attractively proportioned and decorated house could almost make one forget the adjoining vineyard.

265

CHÂTEAU
DAUZAC

Margaux

" Time can be merciless when it's ignored." André Lurton, undeniably one of the foremost vintners in the Bordeaux region, has adopted this pithy maxim by wise old Fernand Ginestet for his own. His past experience has taught him how true it is; Lurton is in a position to understand exactly how much patience, slow maturing, and seizing of opportunity—how much *time*, in other words—is required by any major undertaking. In his earliest childhood, he learned to value things that last from his maternal grandfather, the wise Léonce Récapé. An especially apt philosophy for Dauzac, where swift, violent change has caused undue suffering in the past.

The relevance of André Lurton's philosophy is borne out by the string of châteaux he manages with a success that has made his reputation on several continents and reflects an adventure virtually unique of its kind. This must surely have weighed heavily in the balance when the directors of MAIF (Mutuelle d'Assurances des Instituteurs de France, an insurance company) met in 1992 at their Niort headquarters and decided to entrust Lurton with the reins of

an estate they had been trying for almost four years to put back on its feet.

It would perhaps be an exaggeration to claim that their proposition was welcomed with enthusiasm by the man they had chosen. The Lurton family is too well established elsewhere in the Médoc region for André to have been overjoyed at the idea of adding yet another responsibility to an already long list. But this kind of challenge is hard to refuse, and his desire to meet it overcame his reluctance.

And this is how it happened that—contrary to custom—a great and established vintner modestly agreed to fill a post offered by a corporation. Lurton stamped the project with his own distinctive mark from the outset. When he recalls the 1993 harvest, and his initial attempts to rationalize operations at a vineyard badly in need of a firm hand at the helm, the memory brings a smile to his lips even today.

Now, twelve years later, Dauzac has recovered its former glory; the estate is once again looking its best. Every operation, from pruning the vines to bottling the wine, has been streamlined. Standards are high, and have been

The use of a certain "Bordeaux Mixture" as an insecticide
was first recorded in the pages of these ledgers.

129

Tournées, Vendanges, Voyages

Septembre 1912	Report fs		1.013.40	1.612.90
			206. 0	
			87. 0	
			7. 00	72. 25
			249. 50	

Octobre 1913

Décembre 1913

Août 1914

Septembre 1914

DAUZAC

Rapport du 15 Février...

meticulously implemented. Renovations of the fermenting room currently underway will make it possible to monitor individual batches more effectively than before. Meanwhile, the cellars have been transformed and now accommodate hundreds of new casks arranged in orderly rows. As he guides us through the renovated cellar, André Lurton suddenly frowns: he has noticed that light reflected from the semicircular glass roof spoils the desired visual effect slightly. He gives an order, the problem will be fixed at once.

The new team's goal is simple: to make Dauzac worthy of its illustrious past. The estate's history has been preserved in its archives, and most of these—miraculously—survive, a rarity worthy of note. This unique treasure, currently being catalogued, goes all the way back to the twelfth century and the township of Macau, once an annex of the Sainte-Croix Abbey of Bordeaux. The history of the vineyard itself begins in the eighteenth century, the period leading up to its apogee under the Restoration, during the brilliant era of Jean-Baptiste Lynch.

Prominent among the estate's many claims to fame is of course the 1885 invention by Professor Millardet and estate-manager Ernest David of the celebrated *bouillie bordelais*. This concoction, a solution combining copper sulfate and lime that is still used today, was instrumental in saving European vineyards from devastating attacks of American mildew. It was surely not pure chance that led to its invention at Dauzac, for the estate has always been an innovating, technologically fruitful enterprise where the old motto, "Time can be merciless when it's ignored," is still respected today.

The back of the château has remained almost untouched (right), but the cellars have been completely overhauled (above, left).

CHÂTEAU
D'ARMAILHAC

Pauillac

So much symbolism is attached to certain architectural curiosities, it's hard to believe they were the result of mere chance and not conscious planning. For example, when the Armailhac château was built, the fine 125 acre (50 hectare) vineyard surrounding its admirable park had not yet become a satellite of the illustrious Château Mouton Rothschild. Thus, the fact that the house was never completed (for perfectly good reasons, no doubt) must be accepted as pure coincidence. The surviving façade is so neatly cut in half, it might almost be the prize-winning exercise of an especially gifted architect.

At the end of the seventeenth century the estate was owned by two self-styled ships' pilots of the Gironde estuary, the Armailhac brothers. At that time there were no vineyards on the property; these came later, in the middle of the eighteenth century, under the aegis of a certain Dominique Armailhac. For over a century afterwards his vineyard was enlarged, tended, and improved by his descendants. Then, toward the end of the July Monarchy, it

formed part of the settlement made to "Madame Darmailhac" (*sic*) when she was separated from her husband, then the eldest member of the family. It is to this lady that the vineyard owed its 1855 ranking—as only a *cinquième cru*, to be sure, but a proud one nonetheless. The vineyard covered 175 acres (70 hectares) lying between Bran-Mouton and Pibran.

This lady's son-in-law, the Comte de Ferrand, purchased the property—until then owned jointly by the heirs to her estate—at the beginning of the Third Republic. He made such improvements to the property as his limited means allowed, but was unfortunately unable to complete the large manor house intended to reflect its eminent reputation. It was thus a "half-château" that attracted the interest of Baron Philippe de Rothschild in the early 1930s. This youthful and dynamic entrepreneur, who had brilliantly guided the destinies of Mouton since 1924, started by acquiring a minority share in Armailhac and then in 1933 purchased it outright from the Comte de Ferrand through

Here, the photographer's skill comes to the aid of the imagination,
giving some idea of what the completed house might have looked like.

an arrangement whereby the latter would be allowed to continue living on it for the duration of his life. When the Comte de Ferrand died the following year, Baron Philippe became the sole owner of a top-ranking vineyard (on the supplementary 1855 listing); a winery he subsequently enlarged in order to accommodate installations suitable for processing grapes from both of his vineyards; and a fine, tree-shaded, attractively landscaped park dotted with beds of camellias. This was exactly the natural backdrop Mouton Rothschild had lacked until then. Included in the sale was the modest Société Vinicole de Pauillac, which was to become—in a different form and with large infusions of capital—the Baron Philippe de Rothschild Corporation.

Following World War II, and for twenty years thereafter, the "half-château" of Armailhac served as the residence of the general manager of the baron's wine-producing estates. In 1956 the great wine made at Armailhac was named after Baron Philippe himself. Then, in homage to Pauline de Rothschild, the name on the labels was changed to "Château Mouton Baronne Philippe." In 1989 Baroness Philippine decided to restore the original name to this great Pauillac wine that had been in the Armailhac family for so long. "Château d'Armailhac" is back again, on a label decorated with an eighteenth-century figurine in Nevers cut-glass representing Bacchus—a subtle allusion to the fact that the original objet d'art is part of the collections of the Museum of Wine in Art at Mouton Rothschild.

The vast anteroom to the cellars, with its large shields and fine Bacchus set against an apple-green background in one corner. A perfect example of the daring originality found in the décor at Mouton Rothschild.

CHÂTEAU
DU TERTRE

Margaux

Great wine estates are like people: some have commonplace lives, others follow a nobler destiny. Estates protected by their own lucky star can go through terrible times and emerge from the ordeal unscathed, sometimes even stronger and finer than before. The Château du Tertre is obviously one of these, its stubborn powers of resistance withstanding the direst onslaughts. In just a few years it has risen from its ashes, exhibiting a splendor that, to be honest, it had never known before.

This little hillock has had so many owners since the Middle Ages that a list of their names would rival Leporello's in length. To confine ourselves to the most important, we should at least mention Thomas de Montaigne (brother of the great philosopher) in the sixteenth century; the Marquis de Ségur, illustrious "Prince of the Vines," at the end of the seventeenth; Pierre Mitchell, leading Bordelais bottle-manufacturer, in the eighteenth; and Heinrich Koenigswater, ambassador of Saxony, in the nineteenth. In the twentieth century the property was acquired by the de Wildes, a family of wine merchants from Ghent, shortly before being purchased (in 1960) by Calon Ségur native Philippe Capbern-Gasqueton. At this point the estate was in serious decline, its vineyards overgrown and the roof of the house collapsing.

But the château's lucky star was watching over it, and fresh efforts at restoration began to bear fruit. The real transfiguration didn't take place until 1997, however. As in similar cases, huge amounts of money and mountains of love (or vice versa) had to be poured into the project. The miracle was accomplished under the unerring direction of a couple from the Netherlands, the Albada Jelgersmas, who undertook to endow this great, newly discovered wine with a worthy display case.

The buildings housing the winery have been thoroughly renovated inside and out, and the results are both practical and impressive. Visual impact is obviously a top priority, and the new owners even went so far as to add spacious arcaded peristyles to some of the façades.

The estate's resurrection included
major interior redecoration.

The château itself has been not so much restored as recreated. After the main building had been renovated, a completely new wing was added to it. This addition, based on blueprints drawn up in the eighteenth century but never used, is a key element in the architectural harmony of the whole. The grounds have been freshly landscaped, and now include a stunning garden featuring a group of summer houses erected on either side of a lovely pool. The total effect evokes a Gabriel-style hermitage—nature improved by art.

The marvels visible outside are echoed by an inventive and striking personal style within. It can be seen in the Scandinavian—almost Swedish—treatment of bedrooms, corridors, salons, and pavilions. Natural wood is combined with cotton, fine crystal with sublime marbles, pastel tones with rustic designs, and a few rococo furnishings with fashionable minimalist pieces. The prevailing atmosphere is one of supreme relaxation and unpretentious refinement, making this a refuge blessed by the gods, or at the very least steeped in serenity—a truly beguiling spot in which to live.

The Château du Tertre has known hard times in the past, no doubt about it. When one sees it today, however, one would think it had emerged fully formed from a mind filled with the secrets of villas, of vineyards, and of life.

An entirely renovated mansion (facing page), gardens landscaped from scratch (center), tastefully decorated salons and guest rooms—a dream come true for this château (top and bottom).

CHÂTEAU
HAUT-BAGES LIBÉRAL

Pauillac

At the beginning of this century, after returning with her husband from a four-week pilgrimage to Santago de Compostela, Claire Villars-Lurton made an important decision. Henceforth she would stop trying to manage all of her family's extensive properties, and concentrate solely on Ferrière and Haut-Bages Libéral. Here is the kind of choice people make when they've attained a certain maturity. Villars-Lurton, an energetic young woman with sparkling eyes beneath her mop of curly hair, exemplifies a new generation of landowners casting off the unproductive restraints of the past and communicating infectious enthusiasm for their vocation. An extremely positive development.

"Here," she explains, "we don't make a mystery out of the way a great wine is produced. The land returns everything we give it tenfold. I'm continually amazed by the generosity of the Pauillac soil. It's almost too easy!" What our astonished vintner has modestly neglected to mention is the meticulous care given year after year to her vineyard and its adjacent winery. Major architectural work carried out recently on the estate has resulted, among other things, in the addition of two modern and well-lit fermenting rooms—one equipped with cement vats in various sizes—and expansion of the wine cellars housing casks piled to the ceiling, Anglo-American style. The design of the buildings is unabashedly contemporary, combining the slightly grandiloquent elegance of a glass skylight fitted between the cellars with the rough-hewn authenticity of copper siding that will eventually acquire a greenish patina.

Claire's mentor in her craft is one of her uncles, the remarkable Jean Merlaut. This amiable and appealing man is one of his niece's staunchest defenders. As she notes, "He's set the bar very high, but that's because he believes in me. My uncle is totally committed to what I'm doing." Among the many lessons Claire has learned at her uncle's side is, of course, the brand of applied humanism that makes the owner of Gruaud-Larose a compelling leader. "The main thing," says Claire, "is being able to rely on people who are motivated, who love what they do—people who aren't discouraged by the low status accorded to manual work that is characteristic of our times."

A huge tubular canopy linking the two main buildings
anchors the estate in modernity.

It is impossible to overemphasize the importance to a vineyard, generally speaking, of a labor force that is skilled, dependable, and also highly motivated—a major component in the success of any great wine. Access to a pool of skilled labor is such a high priority on this family estate that a training course has been inaugurated for the purpose of stimulating new interest in the field among local workers. "We're looking for people who love vineyards," announces Claire to all comers, "and when we find them, we're happy to help them get ahead. The thing that's a little hard," she adds, "is to see someone we spent a lot of time training hired away from us . . ." A back-handed tribute, perhaps, but a tribute nonetheless.

Thrust at an early age into the male-dominated world of viticulture, Claire Villars-Lurton readily admits that being a woman actually has some advantages, and not only in terms of outside business relationships. Her psychological insight, self-discipline, and intuition—qualities generally perceived as particularly feminine—are perhaps more useful, when all is said and done, than the chemistry courses she once took. Instinct more than book learning. Or, as Barthes defined the Latin word *sapientia*: a little knowledge, much wisdom, and endless zest.

As practiced in Spain and Portugal, stacking casks (facing page) not only saves space but also—paradoxically—reduces handling. Installation of the new winery (bottom) required doubling the building space (top).

CHÂTEAU
PÉDESCLAUX

Pauillac

By late 1996, when the third generation of the Jugla family assumed control of the Pédesclaux estate, this fifth-ranked *cru classé* had lost some of its former luster. Of course the memory of their grandfather, Lucien Jugla, who in 1950 acquired the domain he had managed for almost twenty years, was still very much alive. Lucien Jugla's sterling qualities had conditioned everything on the property. Cautious and astute, even shrewd, this visionary founding father marked all who knew him. He is still the guiding spirit behind the estate; his modesty and open-mindedness are still praised. And yet, Pédesclaux in 1996 was a mere shadow of its former self, and the specter of bankruptcy—narrowly avoided in 1947—still loomed.

The history of most enterprises is marked by cyclical downturns. These are watershed moments, times when difficult and radical choices must be made. In 1996 Pédesclaux was faced with a harsh alternative: sink or swim. The Juglas decided to swim, but they were venturing into deep and troubled waters.

The most daunting challenge was the necessity of waging battles on several fronts simultaneously: management, marketing, methods, technology, among others. But the challenge was met. Brigitte and Denis, typical of a rising younger generation, courageously fought on every front at once. They constructed functional and attractive new buildings. They inaugurated the first "green" harvest. They instituted pre-fermentation maceration, and acquired modern and efficient agricultural machinery.

They conducted their entire campaign—and this is the secret of winning a war—quickly and forcefully. Results were immediate. The 2000 and 2001 vintages revived memories of the wine's best years. The vintages that followed found ready buyers in an expanded but increasingly demanding market.

Today, to their surprise, the veterans of those wars find that the worst of the storm is behind them. The young Juglas are now free to meet less pressing challenges. It's time to focus on cultural projects, on philosophical vision, on

The charterhouse, with its private chapel,
as it was once and will soon be again.

283

creating a new identity. This will of course involve renovation of the château itself, a building unjustly neglected in recent years, whose lovely design and delicate ornamentation could well have succumbed to the blows of fate. Fortunately, however, the building has survived and can still be used to fulfill its crucial symbolic role.

Following structural renovations, Brigitte and Denis plan to restore the five formal suites housed in this emblematic residence. They propose to dedicate each suite to one of the five senses—the physiological means through which we appreciate the good things in life. The idea is an intriguing one, and could help future guests of the château towards a better understanding of the properties inherent in wine that are often only imperfectly perceived: properties that appeal to the senses of touch, sight, smell, and hearing as much as they do to the sense of taste, and that in their artfulness and complexity offer us—despite what some may say—one of the most delightful ways ever invented to embark on a voyage of self-discovery.

Dedicating this estate to the magic of the five senses was a charming idea.

285

CHÂTEAU
BELGRAVE

Haut-Médoc

omogeneous and undivided, the roughly one hundred and fifty acres (sixty hectares) of the fine Belgrave estate are located just within the commune of Saint-Julien. However, through the caprices of official divisions in the wine country, it is relegated to the indisputably less prestigious appellation of "Haut-Médoc." In addition, a certain number of disappointing vintages—reflecting difficulties experienced by the estate following World War II—have tended to foster a less flattering reputation for this *cinquième grand cru classé* than that of its immediate neighbors, a reputation that, since it now contradicts reality, is surely not destined to endure.

Belgrave was acquired in 1979 by the "Vins et Vignobles Dourthe" group, and for the past quarter-century the estate has registered remarkable progress. Progress so dramatic, in fact, that wine critics writing for the international press have for some time systematically ranked this *grand cru* among their favorites, unanimously recognizing the restored preeminence of the estate's production. But Rome was not built in a day: according to the man primarily responsible for this turnaround, Jean-Marie Chadronnier, it was some time before Belgrave found its footing again. There were several identifiable stages in the exemplary process of salvaging this glorious vessel and then steering it to the crest of the wave.

The first stage, lasting until about 1985, was occupied with the basic task of saving the vineyard from ruin and making up for lost time. At that point, the main goal was "to prevent the situation from getting any worse." The only way to achieve this eminently laudable objective was to implement draconian changes in both the vineyard and the winery. "Batten down the hatches and bail," was the new team's desperate but imperative motto.

Next, from the mid-eighties to the early nineties, it became possible to envision "qualitative progress." The first priority was improving the vineyard: installing a much-needed drainage system, providing reasonable protection against pests and disease, fertilizing the soil, pruning the vines and even trimming their leaves according to a particular system. The next stage required outside help, and the

The winter salon, under the placid gaze of heron decoys—one of the house's many charms.

great oenologist Michel Rolland was brought in. This initiative was pivotal. "Rolland is first of all a good friend," notes Jean-Marie Chadronnier when alluding to the advisor who shed a ray of light on a somber situation, "and furthermore, he's a friend whose wine I like."

Chadronnier, the starring player in the drama of the estate's resurrection, adopts a more relaxed tone when he goes on to the next chapter in the Belgrave story, which opened in the early 1990s. With the worst of the storm safely past, restoration work could be started on the château itself—a project that, for obvious reasons, had been postponed during earlier stages in the recovery process. Time passed . . . and Chadronnier brings his story to its climax: "After 1990, we were finally able to concentrate on being winemakers." By which he means that the vineyard—cleansed, rationalized, and returned to its former standard of excellence—can now, finally, benefit from the special care that results in the birth of great wines. "I think I can safely claim," concludes Chadronnier, "that since 1994 at least, we've been making the kind of wines we always wanted to make. We have fewer problems and more options."

The finishing touch was the installation in time for the 2004 vintage of an entirely new winery. Today, it is widely recognized that the quality of this great wine has again reached, if not surpassed, the level it attained at the time of the watershed 1855 rankings. This is eloquent proof of the distance covered over a span of slightly less than twenty years. Such brilliant success invites speculation: might it not be true, taken all in all, that the initial handicap, by concentrating the team's energies on a single goal, was actually an advantage for a château like Belgrave? Perhaps this story bears out the eternal "law of obstacles": those forced to overcome difficulties often aim higher and go farther than they might otherwise have done. The obstacles themselves serve as incentives to supreme effort and, ultimately, to supreme accomplishment.

The resurrection of this great estate also included renovation of the château (right), where, for the purposes of the photograph, a few casks have been placed (facing page).

289

CHÂTEAU
CAMENSAC

Haut-Médoc

We are told that once upon a time the smiling stewardesses of Thai Airlines served Camensac to passengers who asked for red wine. It is also said that this excellent wine once frequently featured on the wine lists of some of the most outstanding restaurants in Northern Europe. Proof, if further proof were needed, that being classified as a Fifth Growth is no barrier to excellent quality. Wine writers, both in France and around the world, are unanimous in their praise of the recent vintages produced by this great Haut-Médoc estate. The wine guides updated annually by some of the best wine specialists in the world regularly list it as one of their favorites. The wine guru Robert Parker, whose opinions in matters of wine, however idiosyncratic, are closely followed by all American winelovers, was unstinting in his praise of the 1997 vintage, calling it "a great success."

The success enjoyed by the Forner family, who took over the estate in 1964, has not gone to their heads. It would take more than a few well-chosen words of praise to shake Elisée Forner, the power behind the estate, from his habitual dignified reserve. His style of management is calm, watchful, but never flustered—qualities he shares with many of the winemakers of his generation, the old school, who are faintly distrustful of the short cuts offered by modern technology. He explains: "What gives such nobility to our efforts is that we work on the margins, on an infinity of tiny details, on aspects that might seem negligible on the surface of things or that less-experienced winemakers might think were insignificant. But you see, no detail is insignificant. In fact, I would even go so far as to say that it is the sum of all these minor details that in the end makes all the difference."

When Monsieur Forner acquired the estate forty years ago, it was in pretty poor shape. He took it on, telling himself that things could only go uphill from there. The vines had been neglected and were not fit to produce wines worthy of their classification. He decided to grasp the nettle and start all over again from scratch, taking advice from the great 1960s oenologist Dr. Peynaud. Dr. Peynaud made a

This unpretentious manor house, the object of successive renovations carried out on incontestably eighteenth-century foundations, offers a serene image in perfect harmony with the spirit of the site.

bold decision that other, less-experienced winemakers might have shied away from. He decided to plant the whole estate with just two varieties—60 percent Cabernet Sauvignon and 40 percent Merlot. His boldness paid off. Camensac owes much of its renaissance to the complementary blending of these two varieties. Elisée Forner says admiringly, and with a hint of nostalgia in his voice, "He certainly knew what he was doing. Dr. Peynaud was a great man who shared the essence of his vast knowledge with us. Unfortunately, there are none like him today.

Today, Camensac has turned the corner. The vineyards have increased in size from twenty-five acres (ten hectares) to around one hundred and seventy (seventy hectares), most of them around the château and along the boundaries with the Belgrave and La Tour-Carnet estates; in other words, it is part of a great wine area. The winemaking facilities are equipped with all the latest technology. Rectangular cement vats have proved ideal for the vinification process. The fermentation cellar is housed in a charterhouse, parts of which date back to the eighteenth century. The building has been lovingly restored and is as beautiful inside as it is outside. Patience has always been Elisée Forner's watchword. He has taken the time to listen to the soil, the climate, and the vines. The renaissance of the Château Camensac label is proof that, given time, constant devotion and sustained efforts will always bear fruit.

Somewhat unexpectedly, visitors to the charterhouse's attractive salons (left, top and facing page) are greeted with a highly contemporary, almost sterile decorative scheme. The Camensac coat of arms, visible everywhere in the cellars (left, center), and several fine trees (left, bottom) add to the picture and restore the balance.

CHÂTEAU
COS LABORY

Saint-Estèphe

"Small is beautiful." In one world—that of *grand cru classé* wine—where an exacerbated sense of outward show all too often tends to favor huge dimensions, vast surfaces, and large volumes, a context in which immense houses, colossal installations, and limitless properties are sometimes presented as so many objects of pride, it is of some interest to note that a number of excellent estates made to the measure of man also exist. These remind us that modest dimensions, as such, are by no means synonymous with mediocrity. The modest dimensions of Cos Labory actually compare favorably with the overweening scale of its immediate neighbor, the other "Cos," Cos d'Estournel.

There is no sensationalism here, nothing grandiose. On the contrary, the extremely elegant but rather small house is still occupied; the winery is far from large, although it has benefited from all the technological improvements brought to the art of winemaking during the past thirty years. The vineyard, measuring a mere forty-five acres (eighteen hectares), contributes to the harmony of the estate, as it does to the moderate, serene, skillful character of its management.

"We're firmly rooted in the earth," declares joint owner Bernard Audoy frankly. "I'm a man of the soil myself. I'd rather be out in the vineyard than anywhere else."

The great wine Audoy's family produces at Cos Labory is less subject to speculation than others and, although its reputation had declined in the past, today it represents some of the best value for money on the market. Not that it aims at mass appeal or facile acceptance. "I don't care much about passing fashion," explains our man, whose diploma from the Institut d'Oenologie de Bordeaux has not affected his basic classicism. "There is a growing tendency, almost everywhere, to increase the proportion of Merlot in blends," he notes. "I'd rather add some Cabernet Sauvignon, which fosters a stronger structure and better aging." In this, Cos Labory is demonstrating more loyalty than others to the traditionally predominant criteria of the Saint-Estèphe appellation—in which the estate is included.

"People appreciate our simplicity," insists Bernard Audoy, going on to point out that the most important virtue for a good vintner is humility. A humility perpetuated

There is something of the traditional Tours-style residence in this charming manor built to human scale—
a discreet and noble neighbor of the phantasmagoric château d'Estournel.

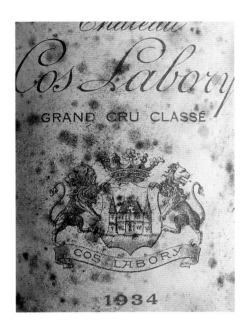

here ever since the day in 1922 when the new owners of the estate, who were Argentineans, sent one of their relatives—George Weber—to France as manager of the property. Weber's daughter Cécile, who married François Audoy, purchased Cos Labory in 1959 from her South American cousins. A happy story with a happy ending: Bernard Audoy is Cécile's son.

Does the benign influence reigning over the property derive from its origins? Or does it reflect a more deeply rooted attitude in which the qualities of discretion, wisdom, and proportion are a perfect match for the estate's (apparent rather than real) austerity? Today, in any case—in an era otherwise permeated with the cheap appeal of clever trickery—Cos Labory maintains a certain sense of moderation, rigor, and rationality which, one cannot help but think, should serve as a lesson to others.

Here is a "model winery"—one which deserves the term for its purity, its elegance, and the economy of means used in its design.

CHÂTEAU
CLERC MILON

Pauillac

Among the oddities of the 1855 classification is this Fifth Growth *cru classé* tucked in between two of the greatest First Growth estates, Lafite-Rothschild and Mouton Rothschild. It is hard to imagine a more paradoxical situation than that of Clerc Milon: just picture a delightful country inn serving delicious food, but overshadowed by famous, world-class restaurants on either side! However, the situation does have some advantages, as Clerc Milon wines bask in the reflected glory of their illustrious neighbors.

In 1970, Baron Philippe de Rothschild bought the Clerc Milon estate. While geographically it was just a stone's throw from his own estate, in terms of quality of production it might equally well have been on the other side of the globe. It was an irresistible challenge for the baron to bring to Clerc Milon all the savoir-faire he had acquired over nearly fifty years at Mouton Rothschild. His team got to work straight away, planting new vines, selecting appropriate grape varieties, and ordering all the latest machinery and equipment, to produce a truly great wine. The first thing they installed was a brand new fermentation cellar that was at the cutting edge of technology for its day.

The intensive efforts soon paid off. In just a few years, Clerc Milon was to relive its former glory, once again fully deserving its classification as a Fifth Growth *grand cru*. In fact, the general opinion was that it might not be unworthy of a place in the Fourth Growth category.

Today, Baroness Philippine lavishes her attention on Clerc Milon and the beautiful adjoining property of Armailhac. The superb results demonstrate that the baroness has an instinctive feel for what it takes to produce excellent wines, not just in the perfect conditions of the Château Mouton Rothschild, (but also in the trickier conditions of their other estates).

It is interesting that the labels on bottles of Château Clerc Milon now feature a pair of tiny figurines dancing a jig, made by a sixteenth-century German goldsmith. These precious figurines, now in the Rothschilds' private museum dedicated to wine in art, are symbolic of the family's joy at bringing a neglected vineyard back to its full potential.

The most elegant charterhouses and most sophisticated wineries
will never achieve the noble simplicity of a plain row of casks.

The Museum of Wine in Art—a brilliant idea of Baron Philippe's—displays a vast collection of the labels used for the family's great wine.

CHÂTEAU
CROIZET-BAGES

Pauillac

There hasn't been a château in Croizet-Bages for at least a hundred years. The estate formerly had a château, built in 1875 on the quayside in Pauillac—something this Fifth Growth had in common with Château Grand-Puy Ducasse—but it turned out to be too far from the vineyard for the owners' liking, and so they sold it. Today, the owners shrug their shoulders and say that it was the Belle Epoque, when marketing and brand image had yet to be invented, and that anyway it is too late now to blame the winegrowers for selling the château so that they could devote all their efforts to their grapevines.

Be that as it may, the sale of the château meant the vineyard was something of a rudderless ship when Paul Quié took it over in 1930. Today, the estate is in the hands of his son Jean-Michel. He makes no secret of his admiration for the old ways and his deep-rooted love of his land. It is no coincidence that his address in the tiny hamlet of Bages is in rue des Vignerons—Winegrowers' Street.

It becomes apparent from the beginning of our visit that Jean-Michel Quié never went in for the fads and fashions of the 1980s—the sophisticated equipment dreamed up by oenologists and the tricks that certain much-admired wine experts swore by for a while. "That sort want to make wine to taste rather than to drink," he grumbles. He believes firmly that by turning his back on fashion, he will find his own way into the wine guides. Croizet-Bages seems to have proven his approach right thus far. It is—dare I say it?—a refreshing change to come across a simple, honest wine that does not give itself airs.

I should perhaps explain what I mean by simple wines. I do not mean it in a pejorative sense in the slightest, as some wines that I would describe as simple are in fact exceedingly complex. Jean-Michel Quié echoes an epigram of Oscar Wilde's, saying. "Trying to bring lots of simple things together can get very complicated."

He shakes his head and sighs over the past fashion launched by a select in-crowd for wines that were softer, less invigorating, and ready to drink earlier. These wines were characterized by their acid fruitiness and very ripe tannins. He is delighted that people are now beginning to return to

The estate's coat of arms reign with somewhat
naïve eloquence at the end of the cellar.

more natural, and much more structured, wines. It is a treat to watch the Croizet-Bages winemakers at work, tasting the mouthfeel of some of their recent productions, eyes closed, cheeks sucked in to extract the last drop of flavor. They love solid, straightforward wines that are nonetheless pleasant to drink. The wines they produce display their provenance proudly. The winegrowers here like to define their work as a cross between farming and geology. They are the first to praise the current trend of getting back to the basics and bringing out the best of the *terroir*.

Jean-Michel and his team have deliberately made much of their recent work, as it has been widely acknowledged that Croizet-Bages still had a lot of progress to make. They have succeeded in getting their raw material—the grapes—up to scratch. "We do all we can in the early stages to try and eliminate chance from the process, which reduces the risk of unpleasant surprises later down the line." This is the absolute bedrock of winemaking. Without decent grapes, no wine will ever be worth drinking But it is the human touch which makes all the difference between an average wine and a good one. Jean-Michel Quié is now concentrating all his efforts on the vinification process. "When it comes down to it," he says, "vinification is like converting a try." (Southwestern France is very big on rugby.)

The château's fermenting vats, some in stainless steel (facing page) and some in cement (top), provide a certain flexibility in grape processing.

CHÂTEAU
CANTEMERLE

Haut-Médoc

If you drive out of Bordeaux along one of the charming roads that wind among the gently rolling hills of the Médoc, the sight of Cantemerle will inevitably persuade you to stop for a visit. Cantemerle is one of the first *grands crus classés* on the road out of Bordeaux. Its imposing gates are easily seen from the road; driving through them will bring you into large parklands dotted with venerable old trees, with the château in the distance. It is a delightful prospect.

Philippe Dambrine is the manager of the Cantemerle estate, which now belongs to an insurance company. He can often be seen out and about in his off-road vehicle in the vineyards, as on this gray, drizzly winter's day, when he was making one of his regular inspections of the grapevines, kept in perfect condition all year round. There were a number of employees carrying out off-season tasks in the vineyards, pruning the vine shoots and grinding up the offcuts. "Something always needs doing in a vineyard," Philippe smiles.

Cantemerle has some 215 acres (87 hectares) of vines divided into three roughly equal parts, which are occasionally left fallow to rest the soil before being replanted with a different grape variety. "It gives the soil a chance to breathe and to get its strength back. You know, vineyards are like living creatures."

Nowadays, the fashion is for rediscovering the old ways and traditional techniques, after a decade or two when modern technology was seen as the way forward. The great wine specialists have all come round to acknowledging the limits of their art, realizing that if the basic ingredients—the grapes—are not up to scratch, then all the technology in the world won't help. Hence the trend back to lavishing care on the vines to produce the best possible grapes. Philippe Dambrine says, "The drive to produce vast quantities of grapes has thankfully long since given way to the demand for extremely high quality. As far as we're concerned, yield is far from being our primary concern when we're looking at grape varieties."

If space allowed, it would be fascinating to look at the factors behind Philippe's decisions concerning the long-term management of the estate. Among the factors are

The various outbuildings present
a strangely linear profile.

administrative issues such as the "plantation rights" that owners can arrange to transfer from one estate to another more favorable one. Questions might also be raised about the limits inherent in the 1855 classification, as sometimes the reputation of the estate played as great a part as the true nature of the soil.

Philippe Dambrine has had to deal with such problems at Cantemerle. "One of the major difficulties we have had to face was the absence of the main estate archives. Somewhere along the line, the information has been lost, which means we have had to relearn everything by ourselves, yard by yard, season by season. And then you need time to be able to step back and look at the results."

The farther from the château and the outbuildings you are, the more harmonious the ensemble appears. The history of the site becomes apparent. You can see that here there used to be a river port, there a medieval motte and bailey castle. The landscape still bears the scars of the railway that cut across these lands in the nineteenth century.

You will not find the soul of Cantemerle in the storehouses and the fermentation cellars, however efficient. The soul of Cantemerle is right here, in the old vines laid bare in winter's chilly grasp, which speak volumes about the tender care lavished on them for generations past by the people of the Médoc.

Despite the ravages of the 1999 hurricane,
the estate still boasts some magnificent trees.

150 VINTAGES

Below is a list of 150 vintages—including two outstanding ones preceding the 1855 classification—
recognized for their diversity and exceptional aging powers.
This list was compiled from the archives of the Bordeaux wine brokerage firm Tastet & Lawton,
which was founded in 1740 and has kept records of each year's vintage ever since.

1798. Start of harvest: September 13.
Yield: Fairly large.
Quality: Marvelous.
Comments: A benchmark vintage for twenty years;
smooth, rounded, full-bodied wines.

1811. Start of harvest: September 14.
Yield: Satisfactory.
Quality: Exceptional.
Comments: Remarkable wines, dubbed "Wines of
the Comet."

1855. Start of harvest: October.
Yield: Very small.
Quality: Fair.
Comments: Wines considered good in general.

1856. Start of harvest: October 1.
Yield: Very small.
Quality: Poor to fair.
Comments: Acceptable wines, considered by some
experts to contain detectable traces of vine mildew.

1857. Start of harvest: September 20.
Yield: Not large.
Quality: Mediocre.
Comments: Very ordinary wines.

1858. Start of harvest: September 20.
Yield: Fairly large.
Quality: Very good.
Comments: Refined and elegant wines.

1859. Start of harvest: September 23.
Yield: Not large.
Quality: Mediocre.
Comments: Detectable traces of vine mildew in
some of the wines.

1860. Start of harvest: September 26.
Yield: Large.
Quality: Poor.
Comments: Very light wines.

1861. Start of harvest: September 22.
Yield: Very small.
Quality: Good.
Comments: Freeze on May 6. Good, elegant wines.

1862. Start of harvest: September 20.
Yield: Fairly large.
Quality: Mediocre.
Comments: Lackluster year.

1863. Start of harvest: September 23.
Yield: Relatively small.
Quality: Mediocre.
Comments: Some of this year's wines lacking in
maturity.

1864. Start of harvest: September 17.
Yield: Very large.
Quality: Exceptional.
Comments: Exquisite, extraordinarily smooth
wines; mature, aromatic, intense, fully rounded.

1865. Start of harvest: September 6.
Yield: Very large.
Quality: Good.
Comments: Good, mature wines, but harsh;
slow to mature.

1866. Start of harvest: September 21.
Yield: Average.
Quality: Poor.
Comments: Very mediocre year.

1867. Date of harvest: September 18.
Yield: Not large.
Quality: Mediocre.
Comments: Unexceptional wines.

1868. Start of harvest: September 7.
Yield: Fairly large.
Quality: Fairly good.
Comments: Very satisfactory year.

1869. Start of harvest: September 15.
Yield: Very large.
Quality: Very good.
Comments: Remarkable, well-rounded wines.

1870. Start of harvest: September 10.
Yield: Fairly large.
Quality: Very good.
Comment: Very good, very mature, very full-bodied
wines.

1871. Start of harvest: September 18.
Yield: Fairly large.
Quality: Good.
Comments: Light but very elegant wines.

1872. Start of harvest: September 22.
Yield: Not very large.
Quality: Average.
Comments: Lackluster year.

1873. Start of harvest: September 20.
Yield: Not very large.
Quality: Average.
Comments: Terrible freeze on April 28.
Difficult year.

1874. Start of harvest: September 14.
Yield: Very large.
Quality: Very good.
Comments: Very good wines.

1875. Start of harvest: September 24.
Yield: Very large.
Quality: Very good.
Comments: Very good, very elegant wines.

1876. Start of harvest: September 26.
Yield: Not very large.
Quality: Average.
Comments: Wines with reduced aging potential.

1877. Start of harvest: September 20.
Yield: Fairly large.
Quality: Good.
Comments: A year of light but charming wines.

1878. Start of harvest: September 19.
Yield: Fairly large.
Quality: Very good.
Comments: A very great year.

1879. Start of harvest: October 9.
Yield: Not very large.
Quality: Average.
Comments: A lackluster year.

1880. Start of harvest: September 21.
Yield: Not very large.
Quality: Average.
Comments: Vintage comparable to 1879.

1881. Start of harvest: September 12.
Yield: Not very large.
Quality: Good.
Comments: Good wines, hearty and full-bodied.

1882. Start of harvest: September 20.
Yield: Not very large.
Quality: Average.
Comments: Light, fairly elegant wines; some
perceptible mildew.

1883.   Start of harvest: September 26.
        Yield: Average.
        Quality: Average.
        Comments: Light, relatively unappealing wines.

1884.   Start of harvest: September 24.
        Yield: Not very large.
        Quality: Average.
        Comments: Difficult year due to mildew; a few
        great wines.

1885.   Start of harvest: September 26.
        Yield: Small harvest.
        Quality: Average.
        Comments: Many wines affected by mildew.

1886.   Start of harvest: September 20.
        Yield: Not very large.
        Quality: Average.
        Comments: Same problem as for 1885 vintage.

1887.   Start of harvest: September 17.
        Yield: Small harvest.
        Quality: Good.
        Comments: Full-bodied, generous wines; healthy,
        due to antimildew treatments.

1888.   Start of harvest: October 1.
        Yield: Fairly large.
        Quality: Good.
        Comments: Good year, elegant wines.

1889.   Start of harvest: September 29.
        Yield: Large.
        Quality: Good.
        Comments: Satisfactory year, fairly elegant wines.

1890.   Start of harvest: September 29.
        Yield: Average.
        Quality: Good.
        Comments: Fairly good, full-bodied, dark red wines.

1891.   Start of harvest: October 2.
        Yield: Average.
        Quality: Only fair.
        Comments: Wines often lacking in maturity.

1892.   Start of harvest: September 22.
        Yield: Small harvest.
        Quality: Average.
        Comments: Sirocco wind storm August 15,
        temperature 104°F (43°C); elegant wines
        but scorched and often pale in color.

1893.   Start of harvest: August 15.
        Yield: Exceptionally large.
        Quality: Good.
        Comments: Excellent wines that frequently aged
        badly.

1894.   Start of harvest: October 5.
        Yield: Small harvest.
        Quality: Less than average.
        Comments: Poor quality, sharp wines lacking in body.

1895.   Start of harvest: September 22.
        Yield: Average.
        Quality: Average.
        Comments: A year of extremely hot weather;
        vinification difficult; excellent quality for those
        wines that survived.

1896.   Start of harvest: September 20.
        Yield: Very large.
        Quality: Good.
        Comments: Subtle, elegant wines.

1897.   Start of harvest: September 20.
        Yield: Small harvest.
        Quality: Poor.
        Comments: Very mediocre wines.

1898.   Start of harvest: September 23.
        Yield: Small harvest.
        Quality: Good.
        Comments: Slightly harsh wines that improved
        with age.

1899.   Start of harvest: September 24.
        Yield: Very large.
        Quality: Very good.
        Comments: A very high-quality year.

1900.   Start of harvest: September 24.
        Yield: Very large.
        Quality: Exceptional.
        Comments: One of the great years of the century.

1901.   Start of harvest: September 15.
        Yield: Very large.
        Quality: Only average.
        Comments: Wines lacking in body; some vintages
        aged surprisingly well.

1902.   Start of harvest: September 27.
        Yield: Very large.
        Quality: Poor.
        Comments: A particularly disastrous year.

1903.   Start of harvest: September 28.
        Yield: Very large.
        Quality: Poor.
        Comments: A very difficult year.

1904.   Start of harvest: September 19.
        Yield: Very large.
        Quality: Good.
        Comments: Wines that aged unevenly.

1905.   Start of harvest: September 18.
        Yield: Very large.
        Quality: Average.
        Comments: Light but elegant wines.

1906.   Start of harvest: September 17.
        Yield: Small harvest.
        Quality: Good.
        Comments: Exceptionally full-bodied wines.

1907.   Start of harvest: September 25.
        Yield: Very large.
        Quality: Average.
        Comments: Light, elegant wines similar to the 1905
        vintage.

1908.   Start of harvest: September 21.
        Yield: Average.
        Quality: Only average.
        Comments: Slightly harsh wines lacking in charm.

1909.   Start of harvest: September 26.
        Yield: Average.
        Quality: Only average.
        Comments: Potentially good wines that aged badly.

1910.   Start of harvest: October 10.
        Yield: Small harvest.
        Quality: Poor.
        Comments: A particularly disastrous year.

1911.   Start of harvest: September 20.
        Yield: Average
        Quality: Fairly good.
        Comments: A year of extremely hot weather.

1912.   Start of harvest: September 26.
        Yield: Very large.
        Quality: Poor.
        Comments: Wines lacking body.

1913.   Start of harvest: September 25.
        Yield: Very large.
        Quality: Poor.
        Comments: Weak wines with low tannin content.

1914.   Start of harvest: September 20.
        Yield: Average.
        Quality: Only average.
        Comments: These initially promising wines aged
        badly.

1915.   Start of harvest: September 22.
        Yield: Small harvest.
        Quality: Poor.
        Comments: Vintage comparable to 1910.

1916.   Start of harvest: September 26.
        Yield: Average.
        Quality: Good.
        Comments: Hearty, full-bodied wines slightly
        lacking in charm.

1917.   Start of harvest: September 19.
        Yield: Average.
        Quality: Only average.
        Comments: Light, "aromatic" wines.

1918.   Start of harvest: September 24.
        Yield: Average.
        Quality: Average.
        Comments: Healthy but harsh wines.

1919.   Start of harvest: September 24.
        Yield: Very large.
        Quality: Average.
        Comments: Light wines somewhat lacking in
        concentration.

1920.   Start of harvest: September 22.
        Yield: Average.
        Quality: Good.
        Comments: A few good bottles still available.

1921.   Start of harvest: September 15.
        Yield: Average.
        Quality: Very good.
        Comments: A year of extremely hot weather;
        problems with aging. A few good bottles still
        available.

1922.   Start of harvest: September 19.
        Yield: Very large.
        Quality: Only average.
        Comments: Light, flat wines.

1923. Start of harvest: October 1.
Yield: Average.
Quality: Average.
Comments: Pale-colored wines; some wines suffered from the heat.

1924. Start of harvest: September 19.
Yield: Very large.
Quality: Very good.
Comments: Some wines still exceptional.

1925. Start of harvest: October 3.
Yield: Very large.
Quality: Only average.
Comments: Sharp, immature wines.

1926. Start of harvest: October 4.
Yield: Small harvest.
Quality: Very good.
Comments: Some wines still exceptional. Widespread crop failure.

1927. Start of harvest: September 27.
Yield: Average.
Quality: Poor.
Comments: Very rainy August and September; disappointing year.

1928. Start of harvest: September 25.
Yield: Average.
Quality: Exceptional.
Comments: Remarkable wines; some a little harsh.

1929. Start of harvest: September 26.
Yield: Average.
Quality: Exceptional.
Comments: One of the great years of the century.

1930. Start of harvest: October 1.
Yield: Small harvest.
Quality: Poor.
Comments: There are almost no bottles of this wine remaining today.

1931. Start of harvest: September 25.
Yield: Average.
Quality: Only average.
Comments: There are almost no bottles of this wine remaining today.

1932. Start of harvest: October 15.
Yield: Small harvest.
Quality: Poor.
Comments: Vintage comparable to 1930 and 1931.

1933. Start of harvest: September 22.
Yield: Average.
Quality: Average.
Comments: Light, "aromatic" wines.

1934. Start of harvest: September 14.
Yield: Very large.
Quality: Very good.
Comments: A few bottles remain that are still appealing.

1935. Start of harvest: September 30.
Yield: Very large.
Quality: Only average.
Comments: Slightly sharp wines, some lacking maturity.

1936. Start of harvest: October 1–4.
Yield: Average.
Quality: Only average.
Comments: Sharp wines lacking maturity.

1937. Start of harvest: September 20.
Yield: Average.
Quality: Very good.
Comments: Many great wines still available.

1938. Start of harvest: September 28.
Yield: Average.
Quality: Average.
Comments: Unexceptional year.

1939. Start of harvest: October 2.
Yield: Very large.
Quality: Average.
Comments: Light, "aromatic" wines.

1940. Start of harvest: September 26.
Yield: Average.
Quality: Fairly good.
Comments: Unexceptional year.

1941. Start of harvest: October 3.
Yield: Average.
Quality: Poor.
Comments: Very mediocre wines.

1942. Start of harvest: September 19.
Yield: Average.
Quality: Good.
Comments: With 1943, the best year of the period.

1943. Start of harvest: September 19.
Yield: Average.
Quality: Very good.
Comments: A few major successes.

1944. Start of harvest: September 27.
Yield: Average.
Quality: Average.
Comments: Light, agreeable wines.

1945. Start of harvest: September 13.
Yield: Small harvest.
Quality: Exceptional.
Comments: Disastrous freeze on May 2; very concentrated wines, some still surprisingly young.

1946. Start of harvest: September 30.
Yield: Average.
Quality: Average.
Comments: Wines that are often harsh and slightly lacking in maturity.

1947. Start of harvest: September 19.
Yield: Average.
Quality: Very good.
Comments: A few legendary bottles approaching perfection; wines with great charm.

1948. Start of harvest: September 27–30.
Yield: Average.
Quality: Good.
Comments: A few exceptional wines.

1949. Start of harvest: September 27.
Yield: Average.
Quality: Very good.
Comments: Magnificent wines, still capable of further aging; vintage similar to that of 1947.

1950. Start of harvest: September 23.
Yield: Large.
Quality: Good.
Comments: Light, agreeable wines; some very great wines.

1951. Start of harvest: October 9.
Yield: Average.
Quality: Only average.
Comments: Comparable to the 1946 wines.

1952. Start of harvest: September 17.
Yield: Average.
Quality: Very good.
Comments: Well-structured tannic wines, slow to mature; a few great bottles.

1953. Start of harvest: October 1.
Yield: Average.
Quality: Very good.
Comments: A great classic: balanced, full-bodied, subtle, long-lasting.

1954. Start of harvest: October 10.
Yield: Average.
Quality: Only average.
Comments: Healthy but immature wines.

1955. Start of harvest: September 29.
Yield: Average.
Quality: Very good.
Comments: Well-structured, concentrated, slow to mature; a few very great bottles.

1956. Start of harvest: October 14.
Yield: Small harvest.
Quality: Only average.
Comments: Catastrophic freeze in February; little or no production.

1957. Start of harvest: October 4.
Yield: Not large.
Quality: Average.
Comments: Major crop failure; with some exceptions, wines generally disappointing.

1958. Start of harvest: October 10.
Yield: Small harvest.
Quality: Average.
Comments: Average year with some fairly good exceptions.

1959. Start of harvest: September 20.
Yield: Small harvest.
Quality: Exceptional.
Comments: A very hot, dry year; vinification difficult; very great wines with persistent keeping power.

1960. Start of harvest: September 15.
Yield: Average.
Quality: Average.
Comments: Light wines with limited keeping power.

1961. Start of harvest: September 22.
Yield: Very small.
Quality: Exceptional.
Comments: The great year of the century; severe crop loss.

1962. Start of harvest: October 1.
Yield: Large.
Quality: Very good.
Comments: Appealing wines with great charm on the palate; similar to 1924.

1963. Start of harvest: October 7.
Yield: Large.
Quality: Only average.
Comments: An extremely weak vintage similar to 1965 and 1968.

1964. Start of harvest: September 28.
Yield: Large.
Quality: Very good.
Comments: Uneven success; a few great wines with keeping power.

1965. Start of harvest: September 30.
Yield: Large.
Quality: Only average.
Comments: Comparable to the wines of 1963 and 1968.

1966. Start of harvest: September 20.
Yield: Average.
Quality: Very good.
Comments: A classic vintage; great elegance; the best year of the decade after 1961.

1967. Start of harvest: September 25.
Yield: Average.
Quality: Fairly good.
Comments: Agreeable wines; suitable for drinking while still young.

1968. Start of harvest: September 22.
Yield: Average.
Quality: Only average.
Comments: Comparable to 1963 and 1965.

1969. Start of harvest: September 23.
Yield: Small.
Quality: Average.
Comments: Unremarkable vintage.

1970. Start of harvest: September 7.
Yield: Very large.
Quality: Very good.
Comments: Somewhat harsh tannic wines; the best will continue to age beyond 2000.

1971. Start of harvest: September 27.
Yield: Small.
Quality: Very good.
Comments: Extensive crop loss; wines with a somewhat delicate elegance at its most intense in the best of them.

1972. Start of harvest: October 9.
Yield: Average.
Quality: Average.
Comments: Disappointing year.

1973. Start of harvest: September 24.
Yield: Very large.
Quality: Average.
Comments: Generally disappointing wines, with a few exceptions.

1974. Start of harvest: September 26.
Yield: Large.
Quality: Average.
Comments: Generally disappointing wines, with a few exceptions.

1975. Start of harvest: September 22.
Yield: Average.
Quality: Very good.
Comments: Tannic wines of uneven quality; some of them very good.

1976. Start of harvest: September 13.
Yield: Large.
Quality: Good.
Comments: Very hot summer, with losses due to drought; very high quality somewhat attenuated by sporadic rain during the harvest.

1977. Start of harvest: October 5.
Yield: Small.
Quality: Average.
Comments: Freezes on March 31 and April 9; fairly good wines, although tannic and somewhat harsh.

1978. Start of harvest: October 8.
Yield: Average.
Quality: Very good.
Comments: Classic, elegant wines at their very best.

1979. Start of harvest: October 5.
Yield: Very large.
Quality: Good.
Comments: The best of this year's wines are harmonious and well-balanced.

1980. Start of harvest: October 8.
Yield: Average.
Quality: Fairly good.
Comments: Light, mellow, full-flavored wines.

1981. Start of harvest: September 28.
Yield: Average.
Quality: Good.
Comments: Wines that improve with age.

1982. Start of harvest: September 13.
Yield: Very large.
Quality: Exceptional.
Comments: Magnificent wines that will age well into the middle of the twenty-first century.

1983. Start of harvest: September 26.
Yield: Large.
Quality: Very good.
Comments: Full-bodied, often remarkable wines.

1984. Start of harvest: October 1.
Yield: Average.
Quality: Average.
Comments: A generally disappointing year.

1985. Start of harvest: September 30.
Yield: Large.
Quality: Very good.
Comments: Remarkable wines, comparable to 1986.

1986. Start of harvest: September 26.
Yield: Very large.
Quality: Very good.
Comments: A great year for wines with keeping power, especially in the Médoc.

1987. Start of harvest: October 1.
Yield: Average.
Quality: Fairly good.
Comments: Mellow, full-flavored, elegant wines; agreeable to drink while still young.

1988. Start of harvest: September 28.
Yield: Very large.
Quality: Very good.
Comments: Classic wines that improve with age.

1989. Start of harvest: September 4.
Yield: Large.
Quality: Exceptional.
Comments: A very great year for wines that mature with age.

1990. Start of harvest: September 12.
Yield: Very large.
Quality: Exceptional.
Comments: A great hot-weather year; wines suitable for drinking young that also have a high potential for improving with age.

1991. Start of harvest: September 30.
Yield: Very small.
Quality: Fairly good.
Comments: Freeze on April 21. Full-bodied red wines.

1992. Start of harvest: September 29.
Yield: Very large.
Quality: Average.
Comments: Full-bodied red wines that age quickly.

1993. Start of harvest: September 20.
Yield: Very large.
Quality: Fairly good.
Comments: Red wines that age fairly quickly.

1994. Start of harvest: September 16.
Yield: Large.
Quality: Good.
Comments: Classic red wines.

1995. Start of harvest: September 18.
Yield: Large.
Quality: Very good.
Comments: A year of consistent quality. Great red wines, mellow and harmonious.

1996. Start of harvest: September 18.
Yield: Large.
Quality: Very good.
Comments: A great year for wines that improve with age, especially in the Médoc.

1997.   Start of harvest: September 7.
         Yield: Large.
         Quality: Good.
         Comments: Charming, mellow, full-flavored wines.

1998.   Start of harvest: September 23.
         Yield: Large.
         Quality: Very good.
         Comments: An extremely classic year with
         a promising future.

1999.   Start of harvest: September 25.
         Yield: Large.
         Quality: Very good.
         Comments: A perfectly classic year similar to 1998;
         wines with great promise for the future.

2000.   Start of harvest: September 20.
         Yield: Large.
         Quality: Exceptional.
         Comments: One of the great years of the century
         (as was 1900).

2001.   Start of harvest: September 25.
         Yield: Fairly large.
         Quality: Very good.
         Comments: A classic year with great promise.

2002.   Start of harvest: September 23.
         Yield: Not large.
         Quality: Very good.
         Comments: This year's wines were saved by
         the "Indian Summer." Very promising wines.

2003.   Start of harvest: September 2.
         Yield: Small.
         Quality: Remarkable.
         Comments: The year of France's record heat wave.
         A great and promising vintage.

*An extract from the archives of
Tastet & Lawton, wine brokers
in Bordeaux since 1740.*

Notes sur les récoltes de Vin du Médoc depuis 1795

Années	Époque du commencement des Vendanges.	Degré d'abondance de la Récolte	Qualité de l'année
1795	24 Septembre	peu abondante	Très-bonne.
1796	30 —"—	d°. —	médiocre - vins maigres
1797	2 Octobre —	— d°. —	— d°. — d°.
1798	13 Septembre	assez abondante	merveilleuse - citée pend.t 20 ans vins pleins, corsés, veloutés. —
1799	5 Octobre —	peu abondante	mauvaise. —
1800.	23 Septembre	— d°. —	— d°. —
1801	14 —"—	— d°. —	passable. —
1802	23 —"—		très-bonne mais inf.re à 98.
1803	25 —"—		moindre que 1802 toutefois bonne
1804	15 —"—		médiocre —
1805	23 —"—	abondante	— d°.
1806.	20 —"—	ordinaire —	mauvaise —
1807	11 —"—	petite —	bonne —
1808	13 —"—	ordinaire. —	bonne ordinaire —
1809	6 Octobre	petite	très-mauvaise.
1810	19 Septembre	ordinaire	passable. —
1811	14 —"—	assez abondante	des plus remarquables vins dits de la "Comète"
1812	21 —"—	très-ordinaire	— ordinaire —
1813	4 —"—	ordinaire	plate, médiocre.
1814	29 —"—	— d°. —	très-bonne.
1815.	25 —"—	très-peu de vin	merveilleuse - au niveau des 1798 & 1811.
1816.	27 Octobre	¼ d'année abond.te	— Détestable. —
1817	3 —"—	1/5eme de récolte	très-ordinaire. —
1818	17 Sept-bre	demi-récolte	très bonne quoiqu'un peu dure. —
1819	20 —"—	Bonne récolte ordinaire	Parfaite, admirable
1820	30 —"—	Bonne ½ récolte —	Plate, Sans couleur, ordinaire
1821	4 Octobre	moins qu'en 1819	Insignifiante, médiocre
1822.	27 Août —	Très-ordinaire	Sèche, mais bonne cependt.
1823	7 Octobre —	— d°. —	Sans couleur, Sans valeur, Sans réputation d'abord: plus tard un grand succès d'élégance bien mérité.
1824	4 — d°. —	Très peu de vin —	— mauvaise —
1825	11 Septembre	ordinaire (crayon gris)	grande réputation, un peu Surfaite
1826	20 —"—	assez abondante	— médiocre.
1827	20 —"—	abondante	très-bon vin. —
1828	15 —"—	ordinaire	non apprécié au début est devenu une très grande année plein d'h......

Addresses

271 **CHÂTEAU D'ARMAILHAC**
33250 Pauillac · France
Tel.: + 33 (0)5.56.73.20.20
Fax: + 33 (0)5.56.73.20.91
webmaster@bpdr.com
www.bpdr.com

242 **CHÂTEAU BATAILLEY**
33250 Pauillac · France
Tel.: + 33 (0)5.56.00.00.97
Fax: + 33 (0)5.57.87.48.61
domaines.boriemanoux@dial.oleane.com

286 **CHÂTEAU BELGRAVE**
Vignobles Dourthe
33112 Saint-Laurent Medoc · France
Tel.: + 33 (0)5.56.59.40.20
Fax: + 33 (0)5.56.59.40.46
belgrave@cvbg.com
www.dourthe.com

224 **CHÂTEAU BEYCHEVELLE**
33250 Saint-Julien · France
Tel.: + 33 (0)5.56.73.20.70
Fax: + 33 (0)5.56.73.20.71
beychevelle@beychevelle.com
www.beychevelle.com

162 **CHÂTEAU BOYD-CANTENAC**
Cantenac 33460 Margaux · France
Tel.: + 33 (0)5.57.88.90.82
Fax: + 33 (0)5.57.88.33.27
contact@boyd-cantenac.fr
www.boyd-cantenac.fr

204 **CHÂTEAU BRANAIRE-DUCRU**
33250 Saint-Julien · France
Tel.: + 33 (0)5.56.59.25.86
Fax: + 33 (0)5.56.59.16.26
branaire@branaire.com
www.branaire.com

113 **CHÂTEAU BRANE-CANTENAC**
33460 Margaux · France
Tel.: + 33 (0)5.57.88.83.33
Fax: + 33 (0)5.57.88.72.51
contact@brane-cantenac.com
www.brane-cantenac.com

183 **CHÂTEAU CALON SÉGUR**
33180 Saint-Éstèphe · France
Tel.: + 33 (0)5.56.59.30.08
Fax: + 33 (0)5.56.59.71.51

291 **CHÂTEAU CAMENSAC**
Route de Saint-Julien
33112 Saint-Laurent Medoc · France
Tel.: + 33 (0)5.56.59.41.69
Fax: + 33 (0)5.56.59.41.73
chateaucamensac@wanadoo.fr
www.chateaucamensac.com

306 **CHÂTEAU CANTEMERLE**
33460 Macau · France
Tel.: + 33 (0)5.57.97.02.82

Fax: + 33 (0)5.57.97.02.84
cantemerle@cantemerle.com
www.chateau-cantemerle.com

167 **CHÂTEAU CANTENAC BROWN**
33460 Saint-Julien · France
Tel.: + 33 (0)5.57.88.81.81
Fax: + 33(0)5.57.88.81.90
infochato@cantenacbrown.com
www.chateaucantenacbrown.com

299 **CHÂTEAU CLERC MILON**
33250 Pauillac · France
Tel.: + 33 (0)5.56.73.20.20
Fax: + 33 (0)5.56.73.20.91
webmaster@bpdr.com
www.bpdr.com

128 **CHÂTEAU COS D'ESTOURNEL**
33180 Saint-Éstèphe · France
Tel.: + 33 (0)5.56.73.15.50
Fax: + 33 (0)05.56.59.72.59
estournel@estournel.com
www.cosestournel.com

294 **CHÂTEAU COS LABORY**
33180 Saint-Éstèphe · France
Tel.: + 33 (0)5.56.59.30.22
Fax: + 33 (0)5.56.59.73.52
cos-labory@wanadoo.fr

302 **CHÂTEAU CROIZET-BAGES**
Rue de la Verrerie
33250 Pauillac · France
Tel.: + 33 (0)5.56.59.01.62
Fax: + 33(0)5.56.59.23.39
jphiquie@net-up.com

266 **CHÂTEAU DAUZAC**
1 Avenue Georges Johnson
Labarde
33460 Margaux · France
Tel.: + 33 (0)5.57.88.32.10
Fax: + 33 (0)5.57.88.96.00
andre.lurton@andrelurton.com
www.andrelurton.com

178 **CHÂTEAU DESMIRAIL**
Cantenac
33460 Margaux · France
Tel.: + 33 (0)5.57.88.34.33
Fax: + 33 (0)5.57.88.96.27
desmirail.accueil@free.fr

124 **CHÂTEAU DUCRU-BEAUCAILLOU**
33250 Saint-Julien · France
Tel.: + 33 (0)5.56.73.16.73
Fax: + 33 (0)5.56.59.27.37
je-borie@je-borie-sa.com

209 **CHÂTEAU DUHART-MILON**
33250 Pauillac · France
Tel.: + 33 (0)5.56.73.18.18
Fax: + 33 (0)5.56.59.26.83
www.lafite.com

100 **CHÂTEAU DURFORT-VIVENS**
33460 Margaux · France
Tel.: + 33 (0)5.57.88.31.02
Fax: + 33 (0)5.57.88.60.60
infos@durfort-vivens.com
www.durfort-vivens.com

186 **CHÂTEAU FERRIÈRE**
33 bis rue de la Trémoille
33460 Margaux · France
Tel.: + 33 (0)5.57.88.76.65
Fax: + 33 (0)5.57.88.98.33
infos@ferriere.com
www.ferriere.com

154 **CHÂTEAU GISCOURS**
Route de Labarde
33460 Margaux · France
Tel.: + 33 (0)5.57.97.09.09
Fax: + 33 (0)5.57.97.09.00
giscours@chateau-giscours.fr
www.chateau-giscours.fr

254 **CHÂTEAU GRAND-PUY DUCASSE**
Quai Antoine Ferchaud
33250 Pauillac · France
Tel.: + 33 (0)5.56.11.29.21
Fax: + 33 (0)5.56.11.29.28
contact@cordier-wines.com
www.cordier-wines.com

250 **CHÂTEAU GRAND-PUY-LACOSTE**
Domaines François-Xavier Borie
33250 Pauillac · France
Tel.: + 33 (0)5.56.59.06.66
Fax: + 33 (0)5.56.59.22.27
domainesfxborie@domainesfxborie.com

104 **CHÂTEAU GRUAUD LAROSE**
BP 6 33250 Saint-Julien · France
Tel.: + 33 (0)5.56.73.15.20
Fax: + 33 (0)5.56.59.64.72
gl@gruaud-larose.com
www.gruaud-larose.com

278 **CHÂTEAU HAUT-BAGES LIBÉRAL**
33250 Pauillac · France
Tel.: + 33 (0)5.57.88.76.65
Fax: + 33 (0)5.57.88.98.33
infos@hautbagesliberal.com
www.hautbagesliberal.com

247 **CHÂTEAU HAUT-BATAILLEY**
Domaines François-Xavier Borie
33250 Pauillac · France
Tel.: + 33 (0)5.56.59.06.66
Fax: + 33 (0)5.56.59.22.27
domainesfxborie@domainesfxborie.com

74 **CHÂTEAU HAUT-BRION**
33608 Pessac Cedex · France
Tel.: + 33 (0)5.56.00.29.30
Fax: + 33 (0)5.56.98.75.14
info@haut-brion.com
www.haut-brion.com

142 **CHÂTEAU D'ISSAN**
Cantenac
33460 Margaux · France
Tel.: + 33 (0)5.57.88.35.91
Fax: + 33 (0)5.57.88.74.24
issan@chateau-issan.com
www.chateau-issan.com

138 **CHÂTEAU KIRWAN**
Cantenac
33460 Margaux · France
Tél: + 33 (0)5.57.88.71.00
Fax: + 33 (0)5.57.88.77.62
mail@chateau-kirwan.com
www.chateau-kirwan.com

42 **CHÂTEAU LAFITE-ROTHSCHILD**
33250 Pauillac · France
Tel.: + 33 (0)5.56.73.18.18
Fax: + 33 (0)5.56.59.26.83
www.lafite.com

220 **CHÂTEAU LAFON-ROCHET**
33180 Saint-Éstèphe · France
Tel.: + 33 (0)5.56.59.32.06
Fax: + 33 (0)5.56.59.72.43
lafon@lafon-rochet.com
www.lafon-rochet.com

146 **CHÂTEAU LAGRANGE**
33250 Saint-Julien · France
Tel.: + 33 (0)5.56.73.38.38
Fax: + 33 (0)5.56.59.26.09
chateau-lagrange@chateau-lagrange.com
www.chateau-lagrange.com

175 **CHÂTEAU LA LAGUNE**
81 Avenue de l'Europe
33290 Ludon-Médoc · France
Tel.: + 33 (0)5.57.88.82.77
Fax: + 33 (0)5.57.88.82.70
p.moulin@chateau-lalagune.com

151 **CHÂTEAU LANGOA BARTON**
33250 Saint-Julien · France
Tel.: + 33 (0)5.56.59.06.05
Fax: + 33 (0)5.56.59.14.29
chateau@leoville-barton.com
www.leoville-barton.com

108 **CHÂTEAU LASCOMBES**
1 Cours de Verdun - BP 4
33460 Margaux · France
Tel.: + 33 (0)5.57.88.70.66
Fax: + 33 (0)5.57.88.72.17
chateaulascombe@chateau-lascombes.fr
www.chateau-lascombes.com

50 **CHÂTEAU LATOUR**
Saint Lambert
33250 Pauillac · France
Tel.: + 33 (0)5.56.73.19.80
Fax: + 33 (0)5.56.73.19.81
info@chateau-latour.com
www.chateau-latour.com

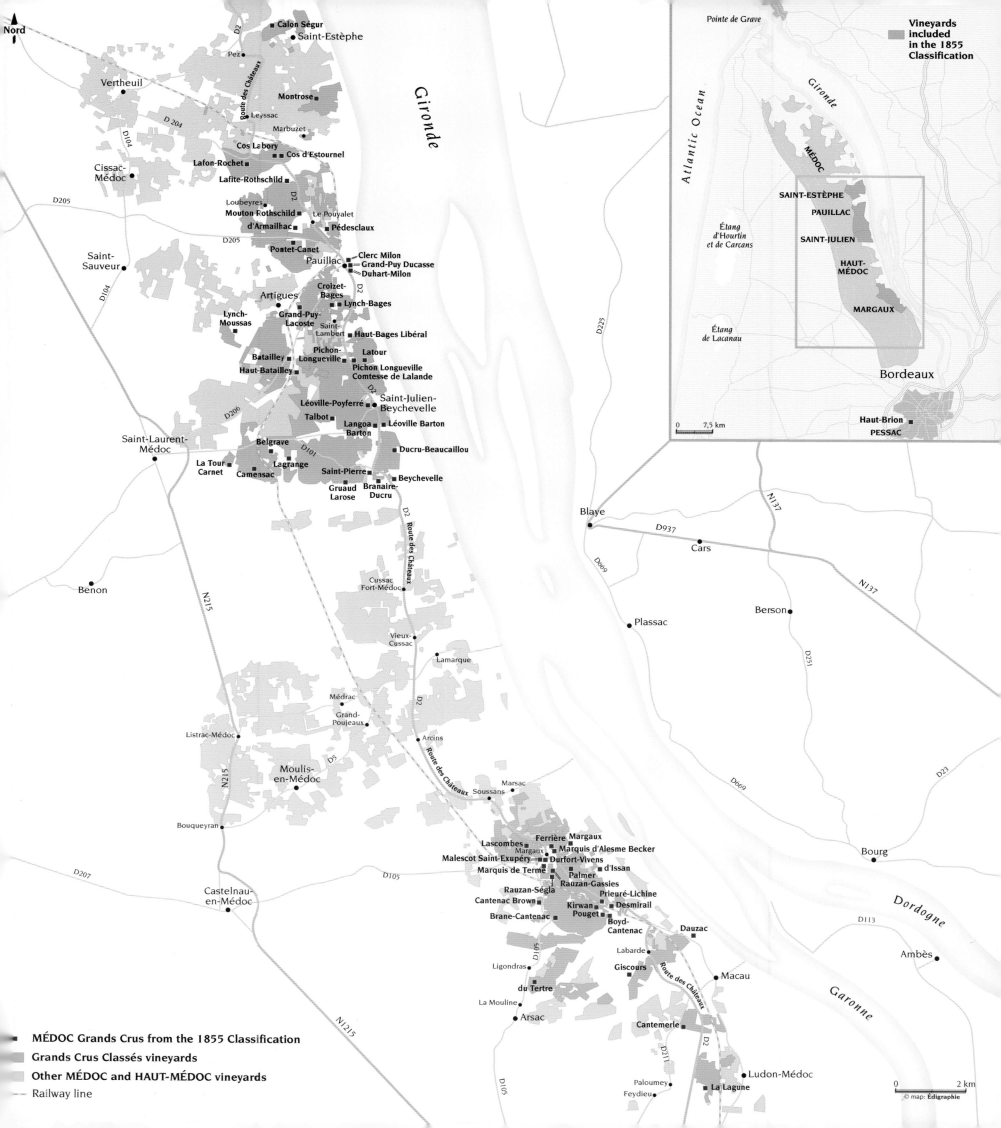

Nord

Vertheuil

Cissac-Médoc

Saint-Sauveur

D 205

D 204

D104

Calon Ségur

Saint-Estèphe

Pez

Leyssac

Marbuzet

Montrose

Cos Labory

Lafon-Rochet

Lafite-Rothschild

Loubeyres

Mouton Rothschild

d'Armailhac

Cos d'Estournel

Le Pouyalet

Pédesclaux

D2

D 205

Pontet-Canet

Pauillac

Clerc Milon

Grand-Puy Ducasse

Duhart-Milon

Artigues

Croizet-Bages

Lynch-Bages

Grand-Puy-Lacoste

Lynch-Moussas

Saint-Lambert

Haut-Bages Libéral

D2

Pichon-Longueville

Batailley

Haut-Batailley

Latour

Pichon Longueville

Comtesse de Lalande

Léoville-Poyferré

Talbot

Saint-Julien-Beychevelle

Langoa Barton

Léoville Barton

Belgrave

Ducru-Beaucaillou

Saint-Laurent-Médoc

D 206

D101

La Tour Carnet

Lagrange

Camensac

Saint-Pierre

Gruaud Larose

Branaire-Ducru

Beychevelle

D2

Route des Châteaux

Benon

N 215

Cussac Fort-Médoc

Vieux-Cussac

Lamarque

Médrac

Grand-Poujeaux

Listrac-Médoc

D5

Arcins

Route des Châteaux

Moulis-en-Médoc

N 215

Bouqueyran

D 207

Castelnau-en-Médoc

D105

Marsac

Soussans

Ferrière

Margaux

Lascombes

Margaux

Marquis d'Alesme Becker

Malescot Saint-Exupéry

Durfort-Vivens

Marquis de Terme

d'Issan

Palmer

Rauzan-Ségla

Rauzan-Gassies

Cantenac Brown

Prieuré-Lichine

Kirwan

Desmirail

Brane-Cantenac

Pouget

Boyd-Cantenac

Dauzac

Labarde

D105

Ligondras

Giscours

Macau

du Tertre

Route des Châteaux

La Mouline

Arsac

Cantemerle

N1215

D211

D105

Paloumey

Feydieu

Ludon-Médoc

La Lagune

Gironde

Atlantic Ocean

Pointe de Grave

Gironde

Vineyards included in the 1855 Classification

MÉDOC

SAINT-ESTÈPHE

PAUILLAC

SAINT-JULIEN

HAUT-MÉDOC

MARGAUX

Étang d'Hourtin et de Carcans

Étang de Lacanau

D225

Bordeaux

Haut-Brion

PESSAC

0   7,5 km

Blaye

D937

Cars

D069

N137

Berson

D251

N137

Plassac

Bourg

D669

D23

Dordogne

Garonne

D113

Ambès

Macau

© map: Édigraphie

0   2 km

■ **MÉDOC Grands Crus from the 1855 Classification**

Grands Crus Classés vineyards

Other MÉDOC and HAUT-MÉDOC vineyards

- - - Railway line

97 CHÂTEAU LÉOVILLE BARTON
33250 Saint-Julien · France
Tel.: + 33 (0)5.56.59.06.05
Fax: + 33 (0)5.56.59.14.29
chateau@leoville-barton.com
www.leoville-barton.com

92 CHÂTEAU LÉOVILLE-POYFERRÉ
BP 8
33250 Saint-Julien · France
Tel.: + 33 (0)5.56.59.08.30
Fax: + 33 (0)5.56.59.60.09
lp@leoville-poyferre.fr
www.leoville-poyferre.fr

259 CHÂTEAU LYNCH-BAGES
33250 Pauillac · France
Tel.: + 33 (0)5.56.73.24.00
Fax: + 33 (0)5.56.59.26.42
infochato@lynchbages.com
www.lynchbages.com

262 CHÂTEAU LYNCH-MOUSSAS
33250 Pauillac · France
Tel.: + 33 (0)5.56.00.00.97
Fax: + 33 (0)5.57.87.48.61
phcasteja@dial.oleane.com

**158 CHÂTEAU MALESCOT
SAINT-EXUPÉRY**
BP 8
33460 Margaux · France
Tel.: + 33 (0)5.57.88.97.20
Fax: + 33 (0)5.57.88.97.21
malescotsaintexupery@malescot.com
www.malescot.com

58 CHÂTEAU MARGAUX
BP 31
33460 Margaux · France
Tel.: + 33 (0)5.57.88.83.83
Fax: + 33 (0)5.57.88.31.32
chateau-margaux@chateau-margaux.com
www.chateau-margaux.com

**191 CHÂTEAU MARQUIS
D'ALESME BECKER**
33460 Margaux · France
Tel.: + 33 (0)5.57.88.70.27
Fax: + 33 (0)5.57.88.73.78
marquisdalesme@wanadoo.fr

233 CHÂTEAU MARQUIS DE TERME
3 Route de Rauzan
33460 Margaux · France
Tel.: + 33 (0)5.57.88.30.01
Fax: + 33 (0)5.57.88.32.51
marquisterme@terre-net.fr
www.chateau-marquis-de-terme-.com

132 CHÂTEAU MONTROSE
33180 saint-Éstèphe · France
Tel.: + 33 (0)5.56.59.30.12
Fax: + 33 (0)5.56.59.38.48
www.chateaumontrose-charmolue.com

67 CHÂTEAU MOUTON ROTHSCHILD
33250 Pauillac · France
Tel.: + 33 (0)5.56.73.20.20
Fax: + 33 (0)5.56.73.20.91
webmaster@bpdr.com
www.bpdr.com

170 CHÂTEAU PALMER
33460 Margaux · France
Tel.: + 33 (0)5.57.88.72.72
Fax: + 33 (0)5.57.88.37.16
chateau-palmer@chateau-palmer.com
www.chateau-palmer.com

283 CHÂTEAU PÉDESCLAUX
Padarnac
33250 Pauillac · France
Tel.: + 33 (0)5.56.59.22.59
Fax: + 33 (0)5.56.59.63.19
contact@chateau-pedesclaux.com

116 CHÂTEAU PICHON-LONGUEVILLE
33250 Pauillac · France
Tel.: + 33 (0)5.56.73.17.17
Fax: + 33 (0)5.56.73.17.28
infochato@pichonlongueville.com
www.chateaupichonlongueville.com

**120 CHÂTEAU PICHON LONGUEVILLE
COMTESSE DE LALANDE**
33250 Pauillac · France
Tel.: + 33 (0)5.56.59.19.40
Fax: + 33 (0)5.56.59.26.56
pichon@pichon-lalande.com
www.pichon-lalande.com

238 CHÂTEAU PONTET-CANET
33250 Pauillac · France
Tel.: + 33 (0)5.56.59.04.04
Fax: + 33 (0)5.56.59.26.63
pontet-canet@wanadoo.fr
www.pontet-canet.com

212 CHÂTEAU POUGET
Cantenac
33460 Margaux · France
Tel.: + 33 (0)5.57.88.90.82
Fax: + 33 (0)5.57.88.33.27
contact@boyd-cantenac.fr
www.pouget.fr

228 CHÂTEAU PRIEURÉ-LICHINE
34 Avenue de la 5e République
Cantenac
33460 Margaux · France
Tel.: + 33 (0)5.57.88.36.28
Fax: + 33 (0)5.57.88.78.93
prieure.lichine@wanadoo.fr

89 CHÂTEAU RAUZAN-GASSIES
Rue A. Millardet
33460 Margaux · France
Tel.: + 33 (0)5.57.88.71.88
Fax: + 33 (0)5.57.88.37.49
jphiquie@net-up.com

84 CHÂTEAU RAUZAN-SÉGLA
BP 56
33460 Margaux · France
Tel.: + 33 (0)5.57.88.82.10
Fax: + 33 (0)5.57.88.34.54

196 CHÂTEAU SAINT-PIERRE
Domaines Martin
33250 Saint-Julien · France
Tel.: + 33 (0)5.56.59.08.18
Fax: + 33 (0)5.56.59.16.18
domainemartin@wanadoo.fr

201 CHÂTEAU TALBOT
33250 Saint-Julien · France
Tel.: + 33 (0)5.56.73.21.50
Fax: + 33 (0)5.56.73.21.51
chateau-talbot@chateau-talbot.com
www.chateau-talbot.com

274 CHÂTEAU DU TERTRE
Arsac
33460 Margaux · France
Tel.: + 33 (0)5.57.97.09.09
Fax: + 33 (0)5.57.97.09.00
dutertre@chateaudutertre.com

217 CHÂTEAU LA TOUR CARNET
Route de Beychevelle
33112 Saint-Laurent Médoc · France
Tel.: + 33 (0)5.56.73.30.90
Fax: + 33 (0)5.56.59.48.54
www.la-tour-carnet.com

For further information:

**CONSEIL DES GRANDS CRUS
CLASSÉS DU MEDOC EN 1855**
1, Cours du XXX juillet
33000 Bordeaux · France
Tel. + 33 (0)5.56.48.47.74
Fax + 33 (0)5.56.79.11.05
crus-classes@crus-classes.com
www.Grand-Cru-Classe.com

Acknowledgments

This book was designed to serve as a reference work marking the 150th anniversary of the 1855 classification of Bordeaux wines, which will be celebrated in 2005. The Conseil des Grands Crus Classés du Médoc en 1855 wishes to extended warm thanks to the publisher, Flammarion, and in particular to Ghislaine Bavoillot for her untiring pursuit of perfection, and to Nathalie Démoulin and Sylvie Ramaut for their kindness and efficiency. Thanks also to the Tastet & Lawton firm of Bordeaux wine brokers and, specifically, to Daniel Lawton and Erik Samazeuilh, for opening their archives to us and authorizing the publication of commentaries on 150 Grand Cru Classé vintages.

Our thanks to François Laforet and Guy Charneau.

Special thanks to Cristalleries Baccarat.

This project is the fruit of very close cooperation between teams in Bordeaux and Paris, both fascinated by the task of describing sixty châteaux all dedicated to a single goal—the production of great wines.

Without the dynamism, enthusiasm, and diplomacy of Philippe Castéja, and without the dedication of Sylvain Boivert, these 320 pages would not exist. Our sincere thanks to them, as well as to Jean-Paul Kauffmann, Hugh Johnson, Dewey Markham, Jr., Cornelis Van Leeuwen, Franck Ferrand, and Christian Sarramon for their valuable contributions.

A big thank you to Katie Mascaro and Jane Riordan who supervized the English version of the work.

Franck Ferrand extends warm thanks to Philippe Castéja and Sylvain Boivert of the Conseil des Grands Crus Classés, who greatly facilitated his research. He would also like to pay sincere tribute to the owners, technical directors, and managers who throughout his visits to the Médoc region welcomed him—often at their tables—with unfailing courtesy and assistance. Limited space makes it impossible to list them all (over 100) by name, but he would like each and every one to be aware of his gratitude.

Christian Sarramon wishes to extend special thanks to Patrick Duruy for his loyal friendship, to Jacqueline Duruy for many delightful Gombaut evenings, and to the entire editorial staff of Flammarion, who "sustained" the project.